Especially for

From

Date

Praise for *Daily Wisdom for the Mommy-to-Be*

"Every child is a gift from God, and the moments of anticipation and preparation are sacred. Pregnancy is also a time of transition, and Stacey has a gift of helping you focus on the One who does not change. Let the Word of God dwell in you deeply with each devotion as you are refreshed on the inside and find security in God's truth. Stacey's insights are timely and guide you toward the joy of the Lord. Rest in God's nearness and feel His comfort as you savor these pages and this glorious season."

> –Jesse Bradley, author, father of four, Senior Pastor at
> Grace Community Church (graceinauburn.com)
> leader, Activate Ministry (activatelife.org)

"*Daily Wisdom for the Mommy-to-Be* is refreshing, personal, and honest. What an enormous blessing for a mother to grow spiritually as she awaits the birth of her child. The prayers are my favorite part, written from the heart of one who's been there. As a wife, mother, and grandmother, I highly recommend this scripture-based, 40-week devotional for new and repeat mommies-to-be!"

> –Clarice G. James, author of *Party of One* and *Double Header*

"*Daily Wisdom for the Mommy-to-Be* is the ideal gift for any woman who is both expectant and expectant. Saturated with truth and encouragement, this daily devotional invites you to anticipate the beautiful journey of motherhood. Along with coffee, *Daily Wisdom* is my favorite go-to baby shower present, because caffeine and truth are the best combination."

> –Bekah Pogue, author of *Choosing REAL*, speaker,
> writer at bekahpogue.com, and Founder of Pasture

"*Daily Wisdom for the Mommy-to-Be* is filled with truth and heart. As our bodies incubate new life, this book will similarly incubate hope, peace, and reassurance in your soul."

> –Mandy Arioto, President and CEO of MOPS International

"As someone who is not yet a mother, I would be lying if I said I'm not worried about motherhood and all of the wonders that come with it. With all of the unknowns and emotions, I know *Daily Wisdom for the Mommy-to-Be* will be my go-to book when the time comes to help keep me rooted in Christ and encouraged in His Word!"

–Lauren Gaskill, author and speaker

"*Daily Wisdom for the Mommy-to-Be* is a must-read for any expectant mom. This treasure trove is packed with uplifting scriptures, spiritual insight, faith-building stories, and a heap of hope that even includes powerful prayers to pray throughout your pregnancy and over your soon-to-be blessing from God. Stacey Thureen gently holds your hand as she helps you discover how to be the mommy God created you to be."

–Chuck Tate, Lead Pastor at RockChurch, East Peoria, IL, author of *41 Will Come*

"Uplifting and insightful, *Daily Wisdom for the Mommy-to-Be* is a wonderful tool for both first-time and experienced moms. Filled with wisdom and encouragement, each week is geared specifically to what an expectant mom needs. It addresses the many ups and downs of pregnancy with sensitivity and understanding and will help all who read it to prepare their hearts for what is to come. A must for all mommies-to-be!"

–Nancilea Foster, mother of five, 2008 US Olympian

"As a mom of five girls, and now a grandmother, *Daily Wisdom for the Mommy-to-Be* will help the expectant mom grow closer to Jesus as she steps out in faith to have children. Packed with scripture and powerful prayers, this 40-week daily devotional book will help you stay focused on your Creator throughout pregnancy and beyond!"

–Sharon Glasgow, author and speaker with Proverbs 31 Ministries

Print ISBN 978-1-68322-443-3

Published by Barbour Books, an imprint of Barbour Publishing, Inc., 1810 Barbour Drive, Uhrichsville, Ohio 44683, www.barbourbooks.com

Our mission is to inspire the world with the life-changing message of the Bible.

Member of the
Evangelical Christian
Publishers Association

Printed in China.

DAILY WISDOM

for the
Mommy-to-Be

Everyday Encouragement
during Your Pregnancy

Stacey Thureen

BARBOUR BOOKS
An Imprint of Barbour Publishing, Inc.

Dedication

To my family, thank you for your love,
support, encouragement, and prayers
and for helping me embrace
the mommy-to-be calling.
To my heavenly Father, I love You!

Psalm 40:3

WELCOME TO
DAILY WISDOM
for the
Mommy-to-Be

Whether you or someone you know is becoming a mommy-to-be for the first time, the third time, or more, consider this devotional a little gift as you count down the days until the baby arrives.

While reading material abounds during pregnancy, scripture also has much to say about birth and motherhood. *Daily Wisdom for the Mommy-to-Be* is a forty-week devotional collection written by a mom for moms. Each daily devotional is part of a weekly theme related to pregnancy—including being redeemed, being stretched, being delivered, being adored, and being called. These daily devotions are paired with a relevant Bible passage, along with a prayer to help you stay focused on your relationship with God and your growing baby. This devotional is sure to leave you spiritually stable and reminded of your security in Jesus Christ.

WEEK 1

Expectant

The time approaches.
You expectantly wait for
the signs and symptoms to
emerge that will confirm
you are pregnant.

A Great Company

For I will bring them from the north and from the distant corners of the earth. I will not forget the blind and lame, the expectant mothers and women in labor. A great company will return!
JEREMIAH 31:8 NLT

God called a young Jeremiah to be a prophet to the nations. In fact, Jeremiah's name means "God exalts." But Jeremiah resisted this calling on his life. He felt inadequate, unqualified, and uncertain of what God had asked of him. He didn't want to do it, but eventually Jeremiah stepped out in faith and received his calling. God told Jeremiah that He'd be with him and that He'd give Jeremiah the words to speak.

Just like Jeremiah, you might feel unqualified or unfit for the calling of motherhood. You may have been thinking about it for quite some time. You may have been resistant, or perhaps impatient. God promises in scripture, as in this passage in Jeremiah, that He will not forget you! He won't even forget the expectant mothers and women in labor!

So whether this is your first, second, third, or more pregnancy, remember that God is with you (Joshua 1:9). You are among the great company of women who view being a mommy-to-be as a calling. With it you get to partner with the best Creator of all: Jesus.

Lord Jesus, as I wait with expectation for confirmation that I am pregnant, help me to remember that You are with me daily.

Sufficient Courage

I eagerly expect and hope that I will in no way be ashamed, but will have sufficient courage so that now as always Christ will be exalted in my body, whether by life or by death. For to me, to live is Christ and to die is gain.
PHILIPPIANS 1:20–21 NIV

The apostle Paul was speaking to the Philippians about the importance of living for Christ. When Christians live for Christ, they live out their purpose to mirror God's image of creation and radiate His glory to others.

It's miraculous how God designed a woman's body. The ability to submit to this design comes with the choice to step out in faith and raise up children. The great calling of motherhood comes with a price, though. Like Jesus, moms die to self too. This isn't a glamorous decision; it's a bold, courageous one. A choice accompanied by the stark reality that over the next forty weeks, and for the rest of your life, you will be thinking not only about yourself but also about your child.

So in these last few days before you conceive, reflect on God's faithfulness in your life. How He has shown you that leading up to this moment He has been exalted in your body since the day you were born.

Lord, thank You for dying on the cross for the forgiveness of my sins. May Your Holy Spirit empower me to live with sufficient courage to pour myself out daily.

Praise Him

*Why are you cast down, O my inner self? And why
should you moan over me and be disquieted within me?
Hope in God and wait expectantly for Him, for I
shall yet praise Him, my Help and my God.*
PSALM 42:5 AMPC

The psalmist was writing a song. A song that would praise God during a time of waiting.

As you wait on God for the news that you are pregnant, praise Him. Praise Him for what He has already done in and through your life and your body. Praise Him for His attributes. Like a mom to her newborn child, He loves you with an everlasting love and sings over you!

Zephaniah 3:17 (NLT) says, "For the LORD your God is living among you. He is a mighty savior. He will take delight in you with gladness. With his love, he will calm all your fears. He will rejoice over you with joyful songs."

So during this time of waiting, whether it is with excitement or concern, choose to praise Him. If getting pregnant hasn't been an easy journey for you, or if you've had multiple challenging pregnancies, commit to praising Him. Praise Him for the courage He's given you to once again give birth to new life.

---

*Father God, thank You for bringing me into this world
so that I may glorify You with the praises of my lips.
Thank You for partnering with me on this journey
of motherhood. I submit to Your will.*

In the Morning

*Listen to my voice in the morning, LORD. Each morning
I bring my requests to you and wait expectantly.*
PSALM 5:3 NLT

The process was grueling, relentless, and exhausting. Faith wanted nothing more than to see the test indicate that she was pregnant. But for the past two years, the answer was no. So she and her husband prayed, contemplated, and begged God for answers. Faith had no preexisting health conditions that indicated she would have trouble getting pregnant. If God wasn't going to provide the answers to her prayers, who would?

One morning, as she woke up early to read scripture, she noted what the psalmist wrote in Psalm 5:3. Faith highlighted the verse in her Bible and decided she would pray with faith and expectancy.

"Jesus, You are the giver of life. I've tried so hard over the past two years to get this right. I don't know why I'm not pregnant yet. But today Your mercies are new. Your grace is sufficient. I can't figure this out. I submit to You and bring my desire before You to birth a child from my womb."

Days later, Faith knew her body had been ready to conceive but she chose not to take a pregnancy test. She chose, by faith, to leave it in the Lord's hands and let it go. The miracle? In her letting go, God gave.

---

*Jesus, I'm waiting on You for the
precious news of this beautiful gift.*

In Due Season

The eyes of all look expectantly to You,
and You give them their food in due season.
PSALM 145:15 NKJV

Psalm 145 is a praise written by David. In fact, it's a song about God's majesty and love.

Verse 16 (NKJV) says, "You open Your hand and satisfy the desire of every living thing."

Did you catch that? David is writing about a God who has you in His hand. A gracious God who satisfies the desire within you. Even the desire to conceive a child. How awesome is that!

Think back over the past few weeks or months leading up to today. Did the thought occur to you that you wanted to bear a child? Did you see a baby in the grocery store and think about how precious and immaculate they were? If you did, God was awakening a desire within you. A desire to carry on the next generation. This was a part of His plan all along. In due season He will help satisfy the desire of your heart to conceive a child (Psalm 37:4).

Psalm 145:21 (NKJV) says, "My mouth shall speak the praise of the LORD, and all flesh shall bless His holy name forever and ever." Meditate on these words and ponder the goodness of God in preparing your body for this amazing blessing.

Lord, thank You for blessing me with the opportunity
to embark on a new season with You. A season of
expectancy, change, beauty, wonder, and miracles.

Waiting Expectantly

*(Anna) came along just as Simeon was talking with
Mary and Joseph, and she began praising God. She
talked about the child to everyone who had been
waiting expectantly for God to rescue Jerusalem.*
LUKE 2:38 NLT

Luke chapter 2 begins with the birth of Jesus and ends with
twelve-year-old Jesus speaking with the teachers.

More specifically, in the text for today, the prophecy of
Simeon comes to pass as well as the prophecy of Anna. A
prophecy is a prediction of what is to come. In verses 25 and
26, the Holy Spirit revealed to Simeon that he wouldn't die until
he saw Jesus.

Anna was a widow and a devout follower of God. As verse
38 points out, she crossed paths with Simeon as he was talking
with Mary and Joseph. Anna praised God for this gift of life
because she understood what Simeon believed: God had a
plan for Jesus.

As you wait expectantly for the news that you are pregnant,
ponder how God has worked all things together in your life for
good (Romans 8:28). Think about how His plan for your life has
unfolded and praise Him for it.

---

*Abba, I thank You for making me in Your image.
Help me to wait expectantly for this baby. As I wait on
You, help me to praise You for the life You have given
me and for the one that is to come inside of me.*

An Unbelievable Inheritance

This resurrection life you received from God is not a timid,
grave-tending life. It's adventurously expectant, greeting
God with a childlike "What's next, Papa?" God's Spirit
touches our spirits and confirms who we really are.
We know who he is, and we know who we are:
Father and children. And we know we are going to
get what's coming to us—an unbelievable inheritance!
We go through exactly what Christ goes through.
If we go through the hard times with him, then we're
certainly going to go through the good times with him!
ROMANS 8:15–17 MSG

In this scripture Paul describes the identity of a follower of Jesus
Christ. You inherit this identity when you receive Jesus Christ as
your Lord and Savior.

In Jesus, you are free from the bondage of sin. In Jesus,
you are born again—a new creation. Regardless of your past,
your place of birth, your upbringing, your childhood, and your
choices, Jesus loves you! When you receive His forgiveness for
your sins, you are forgiven and set free. When you choose to
have a relationship with Him, you are adopted into the family
of believers. You become a child of the most high King!

Jesus, I receive You as Lord and Savior over my life.
Thank You for forgiving me of my sins. As a
mommy-to-be, I thank You for all that You have
in store for me on this side of heaven.

WEEK 2

Conceived

If all goes according to plan, your prayers will be answered this week as you learn that you have conceived a baby!

Miraculous Miracle

*She conceived again, and when she gave birth
to a son she said, "This time I will praise the LORD."*
GENESIS 29:35 NIV

Leah was pregnant for the fourth time, and she conceived another son. The father of her sons was Jacob, son of Isaac. Isaac was the son of Abraham and Sarah, the long-awaited promised son who was conceived—after many attempts—in their old age. A miracle.

Jacob had a twin brother, Esau. But Esau was the firstborn and destined for the blessing from his father. Later in life, Jacob deceived his father, Isaac, and received what was meant to be Esau's birthright blessing.

While Jacob didn't make the best choice by taking away his brother's birthright, God's love, mercy, and grace still abounded in his life. In all, Jacob had twelve sons including Joseph, who after years of trial and hardship became the second most powerful man in Egypt next to Pharaoh. A miracle!

No matter what you have walked through in life, God doesn't discriminate against your upbringing. Regardless of how qualified or unqualified you might feel to become a mommy-to-be, remember God loves making miraculous miracles out of pain, loss, and hardship.

---

*Lord, You are in control of my life and this baby's life.
When I'm tempted to dwell on the hardships I've
endured, help me to choose to praise You. Thank You
that on the other side of a trial is always a miracle!*

Unfailing Love

*For I was born a sinner—yes, from the moment my
mother conceived me. But you desire honesty
from the womb, teaching me wisdom even there.*
PSALM 51:5–6 NLT

The psalmist David wrote Psalm 51 after committing adultery
with Bathsheba. Like a journal entry, his psalm became a poi-
gnant opportunity for reflection and repentance before the
Lord. David asked God for mercy and forgiveness. Even more
so, David was humble. He recognized that his failures and
imperfections as a human being had been a part of him ever
since he was first conceived inside his mother's womb.

God knows your imperfections and limitations too. That's
why He sent Jesus to die on the cross for the forgiveness of
sins. He loves you with an unfailing love; unconditional with
no strings attached!

So as you think about conceiving in your womb, consider
how much God loves this baby. Being a mom is a calling. A
calling that doesn't require perfection, but rather the presence
of the Holy Spirit at work within your weaknesses. Yield to that
truth and God will provide all of the wisdom and insight you
need to be the best mommy you can be for this baby!

---

*Jesus, I'm weak, and I know I won't be a perfect
mom to this baby. Because of Your grace and mercy,
You can provide me with the best wisdom and counsel
to be everything that this child needs. Please help me
to point this child to the most-needed One—You!*

Persistent in Prayer

So in the course of time Hannah became pregnant
and gave birth to a son. She named him Samuel,
saying, "Because I asked the LORD for him."
1 SAMUEL 1:20 NIV

Hannah prayed. She prayed before the Lord and was persistent in her words. Very persistent. In her humility, she waited and prayed for the Lord to bless her with a son. As Psalm 27:14 exhorts, Hannah waited patiently for the Lord. In doing so she was brave and courageous.

Perhaps, like Hannah, you understand what it means to wait patiently on the Lord to conceive a baby. In the waiting you have continued to be persistent in your prayers. As you have brought your requests before the Lord, you have wavered. You have doubted. You have wondered when all this will happen, or if it even will. Perhaps in the waiting a well-meaning loved one has questioned you like Hannah's husband, Elkanah, did in 1 Samuel 1:8.

Now is the time to continue to pray. Keep on praying, like the persistent widow (Luke 18:1–8) who continued to pray. Recall how Jesus invites us to pray (Matthew 7:7–8). God hears you, and He will answer.

Lord, help me to continue to pray as I wait for confirmation that I've conceived a child. Thank You for comforting me with Your peace as I pour myself out to You the same way Hannah did. Thank You for letting me come to You and ask.

His Child First

*After sacrificing the bull, they brought the boy to Eli.
"Sir, do you remember me?" Hannah asked. "I am
the very woman who stood here several years ago
praying to the LORD. I asked the LORD to give me this boy,
and he has granted my request. Now I am giving him
to the LORD, and he will belong to the LORD his whole life."
And they worshiped the LORD there.*
1 SAMUEL 1:25–28 NLT

When Samuel finally arrived into the world, Hannah continued to praise God for her son. She was mindful of the fact that while she was Samuel's mother, he was a gift from God. In fact, the name Samuel means "asked of God." Samuel may have been Hannah's son, but most importantly he was God's child first.

Hannah brought Samuel to Eli. Prior to conceiving Samuel, Hannah had visited Eli at the Tabernacle. Eli was a priest there, and Hannah made a vow that if God gave her a son, she would dedicate his life to the Lord.

Consider your life as well as that of the baby you will conceive. While this baby will be your child, they are a gift from God. They are a blessing to this world and to everyone they will cross paths with. God delights in you because you are His child first.

---

*Father, I look forward to when I get to see Your
child's first cry, first breath, first smile, first laugh.
Thank You for entrusting me with this little one's life.*

God-News

Hannah prayed: I'm bursting with GOD-news! I'm walking on air. . . . The barren woman has a houseful of children.
1 SAMUEL 2:1, 5 MSG

According to 1 Samuel 1:5–6, the Lord had closed Hannah's womb. But later in the chapter Hannah was rejoicing because she had conceived Samuel. In 1 Samuel 2, she prayed a beautiful prayer. A prayer that praised God for what He had done in and through her body and soul.

Even though Hannah dedicated Samuel to the Lord, like she said she would, the Lord saw her faithfulness and blessed her with even more children. The Lord saw her patient endurance to conceive Samuel and her sacrifice in dedicating him to the Lord. In God's goodness He rewarded Hannah's obedience with a houseful of children.

Whether you are conceiving your first, second, third, or more child, God loves this precious little one. It's hard to fathom how He can love all of His children the way that He does; housefuls upon housefuls. So when He blesses His children with the ability to conceive again and again, then—as a mommy-to-be—you get to experience that His love is truly limitless, endless, and unconditional. That's God-news!

Father, You are holy and worthy of my praise. Thank You for setting Hannah apart as an example of what it means to be a faithful, obedient mother. Help me to see this baby not as mine, but as Yours. Help me to love and raise this baby the way You want me to.

In His Presence

*Eli would bless Elkanah and his wife, saying, "May the
Lord give you children by this woman to take the place of
the one she prayed for and gave to the Lord." Then they
would go home. And the Lord was gracious to Hannah;
she gave birth to three sons and two daughters. Meanwhile,
the boy Samuel grew up in the presence of the Lord.*
1 SAMUEL 2:20–21 NIV

Because of Hannah's faithfulness in stewarding the life of Samuel, the Lord was gracious to her. She not only bore the life of Samuel but also had more children. As a result of her obedience, Samuel grew up in the presence of the Lord.

As a mom, she must have been grateful. After having closed Hannah's womb, God opened it up to radiate His glory by allowing her to bear His image into this world. God was in control, and she submitted to His presence and authority in her life.

Luke 12:48 (NIV) says, "From everyone who has been given much, much will be demanded; and from the one who has been entrusted with much, much more will be asked."

To be a mommy-to-be is a high calling. One that demands a lot of time, attention, and responsibility. When you acknowledge Christ's presence, He is always with you.

---

*Gracious Father, thank You for the high
calling of motherhood. I'm so grateful to
be a part of Your design to create life.*

Conceived in Her

*But while he thought about these things, behold, an angel
of the Lord appeared to him in a dream, saying, "Joseph,
son of David, do not be afraid to take to you Mary your
wife, for that which is conceived in her is of the Holy Spirit."*
MATTHEW 1:20 NKJV

When Joseph learned that his soon-to-be wife, Mary, was pregnant, he thought about not marrying her. He was confused. But when the angel appeared to him and told him not to be afraid, Joseph's doubt turned to trust. He decided to proceed with the marriage and trust God with Mary.

Joseph must have felt perplexed by how Mary conceived. As the angel said, the baby had been conceived by the Holy Spirit—a miracle that couldn't be explained. Even today, God continues to perform miracles by helping a woman become a mommy-to-be.

For you to conceive is a miracle. Consider the challenges you may have gone through leading up to this point in your pregnancy. Perhaps you haven't dealt with many challenges to conceive, but you probably know someone who has. Every conception is a miracle, a work of God.

---

*Lord, thank You for helping me to conceive a baby.
Although small and very tiny inside of my womb, this baby
is already a living human being. This baby is already a work
of Your hands. Thank You for this miracle and gift of life.*

WEEK 3

Born Again

Your baby is inside your womb!
You may or may not notice
anything different physically,
but this living human being is
already starting to grow rapidly as
it waits to be born into this world.

Indestructible

*For you have been born again, not of
perishable seed, but of imperishable,
through the living and enduring word of God.*
1 Peter 1:23 NIV

Peter was one of Jesus' twelve disciples who had a strong faith. Peter was a catalyst who helped spread the good news of Jesus Christ to the nations.

But Peter showed his imperfections too. After Jesus was seized and later crucified, Peter denied knowing him three times. Jesus had predicted this would happen. But guess what? Although Peter's denial of Jesus brought him much sadness, God forgave him and gave him a fresh start. As a result of being born again in the faith, Peter lived out his name, which means "rock." He became a man of indestructible faith. Although Peter's denial of Jesus was disheartening, that mistake didn't stop God from fulfilling the resurrection of Jesus!

Currently, the cells inside your womb are a literal and figurative representation of new life. There is a baby inside of you that is just starting to grow. Over the next several weeks your baby will change in preparation for living outside the comfort of your womb. This is a great illustration of what it means to be born into the physical world as well as born again spiritually.

---

*Heavenly Father, You are the author and giver of life.
Although this baby is very small, You are an awesome
and big God! This week, help me to understand
what it means to be born again in You!*

Born Again?

Jesus replied, "Very truly I tell you, no one can see the kingdom of God unless they are born again." "How can someone be born when they are old?" Nicodemus asked. "Surely they cannot enter a second time into their mother's womb to be born!" Jesus answered, "Very truly I tell you, no one can enter the kingdom of God unless they are born of water and the Spirit. Flesh gives birth to flesh, but the Spirit gives birth to spirit. You should not be surprised at my saying, 'You must be born again.' The wind blows wherever it pleases. You hear its sound, but you cannot tell where it comes from or where it is going. So it is with everyone born of the Spirit."
JOHN 3:3–8 NIV

Being born again didn't make a lot of sense to Nicodemus. It was hard for him to understand that a person older than a baby could be born again.

Like a newborn leaving its mother's womb through the birth canal in order to be born into this world, by accepting Jesus as your Lord and Savior you leave an old way of life to begin a new one. If you have accepted Jesus into your life, celebrate! If you haven't, then consider this prayer:

Lord, I believe that You died on the cross for the forgiveness of my sins. Please forgive me. I accept You into my life and desire to have a relationship with You.

Content

Blessed and fortunate and happy and spiritually prosperous (in that state in which the born-again child of God enjoys His favor and salvation) are those who hunger and thirst for righteousness (uprightness and right standing with God), for they shall be completely satisfied!

MATTHEW 5:6 AMPC

To be completely satisfied is to be content. Contentment is being satisfied with who you are and what you have, not wanting more.

Like a baby who thirsts for their mother's milk, you too have a hunger. Yes, you might experience an increased appetite during pregnancy. But your life circumstances might also stir a hunger for possessions or achievements.

What does Jesus say in His Sermon on the Mount about this type of appetite? To focus on the things of Him that are from Him. To turn your attention toward and crave the things that strengthen your relationship with Jesus Christ. When you remember your salvation, that is where you will find true contentment in this life and in the life to come waiting for you in heaven.

Lord, being a mommy-to-be is like a mixed bag of apples from the grocery store. Sometimes the idea of being pregnant tastes sweet to my soul. Other times it seems like there might be bruises along the way, or tough skin is needed. Help me to be content in You no matter what this journey brings my way.

New Creation

*Therefore, if anyone is in Christ, he is a new
creation; old things have passed away;
behold, all things have become new.*
2 CORINTHIANS 5:17 NKJV

Jessica was tense. She and her husband were working with a fertility doctor. The past year hadn't been an easy road for them. They already had one child and wanted more. Getting pregnant with their first child seemed easy compared to what they had been walking through the second time around.

The morning that Jessica was about to drive to a clinic for some tests to determine if she had conceived, she got an email from a close friend who had been praying for her. Her friend mentioned 2 Corinthians 5:17. Jessica looked it up in her Bible. The text stood out to her in a way it never had before. In that moment Jessica chose to believe that whether or not God decided to create life in her, He was using this situation as a way to strengthen her faith.

Maybe you have been walking through some challenges in order to get pregnant. No matter what the end results may indicate, God is using this season to birth new spiritual life in you. Keep your eyes fixed on Him!

Father, You are the author and giver of life. Thank You for making me a new creation through the gift of Your Son, Jesus Christ. Thank You for creating new life within me.

Alive!

*At the time God made Earth and Heaven, before
any grasses or shrubs had sprouted from the ground—
God hadn't yet sent rain on Earth, nor was there
anyone around to work the ground (the whole Earth
was watered by underground springs)—God formed
Man out of dirt from the ground and blew into his nostrils
the breath of life. The Man came alive—a living soul!*
GENESIS 2:5–7 MSG

The book of Genesis begins with the creation of heaven and earth. The text articulates God's majesty, splendor, and detailed creativity.

It was God who first created life. It's amazing that He used the very dirt from the ground to birth a human being! It's awesome how God chose to create life then, and it's still amazing how He creates life today. Through the intricate, dark, delicate depths of a mother's womb God knits together a masterpiece. Although it takes several months before a baby is able to survive and breathe outside their mother's womb, your baby is still alive inside of you.

*Jesus, from the beginning of creation until today,
You are the Creator and Sustainer of life! I'm in awe
of how everything on earth that is alive and breathing
is a work of Your hands! Thank You for creating a
masterpiece on the inside of me and out.*

Heart of God

If you openly declare that Jesus is Lord and believe in your heart that God raised him from the dead, you will be saved.
ROMANS 10:9 NLT

The apostle Paul wrote to the Romans about the saving grace of Jesus Christ. He encouraged them to speak about Jesus as the Lord of their life—that if they believed what they said was true and received Jesus Christ into their lives, they would be born again into new life. These were inspiring words during a time when the Roman culture wasn't an easy place to live out one's faith.

If you are already a mom or becoming a mom for the first time, you may be learning that motherhood is a humbling season of life filled with diverse challenges. There will be days when you may not know what to do, what to say, or how to share your faith. There will be days when you feel like you are at the end of yourself—like you're pouring yourself out, doing thankless work. In those moments, declare Jesus as the Lord of your life. Remember what God did for you on Easter. Recall His heart for you, His unconditional love and mercy that you get to share.

Today I will focus on the beating of my heart. This is a lifeline You created—an image of the love You poured out for my salvation.

Mommy Moments

*For the wages of sin is death, but the free gift of
God is eternal life through Christ Jesus our Lord.*
ROMANS 6:23 NLT

Julia didn't understand why being born again was a free gift. She explained to her friend Amber that she thought in life you had to work for everything.

"That's the great thing about Jesus. When you accept Him into your life and ask Him for the forgiveness of your sins, you become born again. You are saved, and this salvation is a free gift. You don't have to do anything to deserve it."

"Amber, I believe in my heart, and last year I asked Jesus into my heart. I've asked Him to forgive me. But when I think about my children, and another one on the way, and how taxing life can be, I just don't know how to live in. . ."

"Grace?" Amber asked Julia.

"Yes!" Julia exclaimed.

Amber reached into her purse and pulled out a checkbook. She wrote on a check *Paid in Full* and handed it to Julia.

"Hang this up somewhere in your house so you'll see it every day. When you have those mommy moments where you just can't wrap your head around God's grace, maybe because you're struggling to extend it to your kids or receive it from others, think about how Jesus paid it all."

---

*Lord, thank You for letting me be me so that I can be
a mommy-to-be filled with Your grace and mercy.*

WEEK 4

♡

Thankful

Your baby is still very small.
Early pregnancy symptoms may
indicate that you are expecting,
or a pregnancy test may confirm
that you are pregnant.

Think Thankful Thoughts

Let your roots grow down into him, and let your lives be built on him. Then your faith will grow strong in the truth you were taught, and you will overflow with thankfulness.

COLOSSIANS 2:7 NLT

Thanksgiving. Thankfulness. Thankful. What do these three words have in common? They all have the word *thank* within them.

Throughout scripture, one of the core faith disciplines and responses is to be thankful. To be thankful shows that you are making a conscious choice to engage in the art of gratitude. It's not always easy to be thankful. There are seasons in life when the storms rage and the murky mess makes it difficult to see clearly. But when you press through and find something to be thankful for, it will become a beacon of hope.

Chalk it up to pregnancy hormones; there will be days throughout this season when it's hard to feel thankful or think thankful thoughts. Sometimes it takes a step of faith to tell God what you're thankful for. But when you do, watch how it changes your outlook. That murky horizon becomes pure, illuminating the goodness of God.

Father, thank You for turning even my hardest days as a mommy-to-be into some of the best memories. Please fill my mind and heart with grateful thoughts and feelings. Help me to trust that You are in control of my body including my hormones. You have given me a lot to be thankful for!

Always

*Giving thanks always for all things unto God and
the Father in the name of our Lord Jesus Christ.*
EPHESIANS 5:20 KJV

Jackie walked into the bathroom. She unwrapped the pregnancy test and carefully followed the instructions. She could feel her heart beating. After washing her hands thoroughly with soap and water, she exited the bathroom and let the test sit on the vanity counter.

The two-minute wait for the results felt like an eternity. She paced back and forth outside the bathroom until the alarm sounded on her smartphone.

"Okay, God, this is it. Whatever the results are, I will praise You! You know that Jim and I have been waiting for months. I choose to praise You, and I will always give thanks to You!"

Jackie stepped into the bathroom, and before peering over at the pregnancy test, she closed her eyes and took a few deep breaths. Then she opened her eyes and screamed with excitement.

"Thank You, Jesus! Thank You!" she exclaimed as tears ran down her face. In that moment she thought about her family members who'd passed away over the past few years. She thought of Jim and reached for her phone to give him a call.

---

*Lord, thank You for always giving me something to
be thankful for. I'm thankful for the gift inside my
belly. Thank You for babies and the gift of life.*

Dearly Devoted

Devote yourselves to prayer, being watchful and thankful. And
pray for us, too, that God may open a door for our message,
so that we may proclaim the mystery of Christ, for which I am
in chains. Pray that I may proclaim it clearly, as I should.
Colossians 4:2–4 niv

The apostle Paul was giving further instructions to the Christian
community in Colosse. He was encouraging the believers to
be devoted in prayer, as well as devoted to having a thankful
heart. In essence, Paul was spurring believers to be devoted
in their faith; to live wisely even among those who hadn't
accepted Jesus into their lives. He was asking the church of
Colosse to be devoted in all things.

On the day you conceived, you performed an act that
comes with a great responsibility and a high calling. Like becoming a parent, placing your faith in Jesus Christ is a high calling in
life that comes with a purpose and the need to be devoted. A
devoted mommy-to-be, a devoted daughter of the most high
King, and a devoted mom and witness to others.

Jesus, being a mommy-to-be is a humbling experience. It's one
that requires me to be devoted, committed to this call, even
on the days I don't want to or don't feel like it. Help me to be,
as the apostle Paul was trying to encourage the church of
Colosse, faithful in all areas of my life. For Your sake and glory.

Manners, Please

"Mommy, why do I always have to say please and thank you?" Amy asked.

"It's important to say please and thank you because it's proper manners. And people appreciate good manners."

"Oh," Amy responded. "Is it important to God that we say please and thank you?"

Lisa wasn't expecting her five-year-old to ask such a thought-provoking question. At four weeks pregnant, Lisa was starting to feel worn out. All she wanted to do was sleep.

Lisa took a few deep breaths and prayed that God would give her the words to speak to Amy.

"Yes, I do believe that it's important to God that we treat each other well. And part of treating people well is extending good manners. I also believe that God commands us to give thanks."

Lisa walked into the family room and reached for her grandfather's Bible sitting on the bookshelf. Baby brain hadn't caught up with her quite yet, so Lisa remembered to look up 1 Thessalonians 5:18. She read it out loud and explained to Amy that God used the apostle Paul to speak to believers in Thessalonica about the importance of giving thanks.

---

*Abba Father, as I start to feel fatigued during this
pregnancy, please help me to lean into Your teachings
and not my feelings. I need Your help to continually
show You my manners by giving thanks for everything.*

Pious Care

*Let us therefore, receiving a kingdom that is firm and
stable and cannot be shaken, offer to God pleasing
service and acceptable worship, with modesty
and pious care and godly fear and awe.*
HEBREWS 12:28 AMPC

The writer of Hebrews chapter 12 tells about the discipline
needed in a long-distance race. He used long-distance running
as an analogy for participating in the race of faith.

Pregnancy is also like running a long-distance race. Your
body goes through several hormonal and physical changes
to produce a baby that will survive outside the womb. Your
baby's development happens over forty weeks or so; it doesn't
happen overnight. It takes time, patience, and preparation.

When training for a long-distance event, building physical
stamina doesn't happen overnight. It takes several weeks of
training and preparation. It takes, as the writer of Hebrews
acknowledges, pious care.

To be pious is to have a dutiful spirit of reverence for God.
Reflect on the calling to be a mommy-to-be. It does come with
a lot to do. Think about one thing you have to do today that
falls under this responsibility and calling. Commit it to the Lord
and watch how He helps you turn the mundane into worship.

*Heavenly Father, give me eyes to see You in the midst
of all that I'm trying to do in preparation for this new life.*

You Promised!

"Listen to me, all you who are serious about right living and committed to seeking GOD. Ponder the rock from which you were cut, the quarry from which you were dug. Yes, ponder Abraham, your father, and Sarah, who bore you. Think of it! One solitary man when I called him, but once I blessed him, he multiplied. Likewise I, GOD, will comfort Zion, comfort all her mounds of ruins. I'll transform her dead ground into Eden, her moonscape into the garden of GOD, a place filled with exuberance and laughter, thankful voices and melodic songs."
ISAIAH 51:1–3 MSG

Sarah and Abraham were given a promise from God. It wasn't fulfilled until they were in old age.

It took a long time for them to see this promise come to pass. In fact, they even tried—in their own strength—to make the promise come to pass. What was it? God promised that He would give them a son. God promised Abraham that he would have more descendants than he could count! Abraham would be the father of many nations!

You also believe that God promised to give you children. Maybe you have waited a long time to become pregnant. Or maybe you haven't waited that long. Maybe this baby has been a surprise. Whether being pregnant brings you great joy or great tribulation, take some time today to remember that God promises in scripture to be with you!

Lord, thank You for being with me no matter what!

Baby Gates

Psalm 100 is considered a thanksgiving psalm. With only five verses in total, this psalm is about the quality of thanksgiving, not just the quantity of thanksgiving.

Here's how the psalm begins (NKJV):

Make a joyful shout to the LORD, all you lands!
Serve the LORD with gladness;
Come before His presence with singing.
Know that the LORD, He is God;
It is He who has made us, and not we ourselves;
We are His people and the sheep of His pasture.
Enter into His gates with thanksgiving,
And into His courts with praise.
Be thankful to Him, and bless His name.

This week, you may have just learned that you are pregnant, or you are about to find out. Whatever side of the spectrum you are on, take the time to celebrate today! In the months and years ahead, there will be a lot of change. Changes to your body, in your relationships, and even in your home. But all of the change is worth it. Even the babyproofing and the baby gates!

---

*Lord God, thank You for this big change that is about to
take place in my life. You are a gracious and merciful
Father. I have so much to be thankful for, including
this precious gift that You have entrusted me with.*

WEEK 5

Formed

Your baby is tiny, but you might start to notice some early symptoms such as feeling more tired than normal or skipping your menstrual cycle.

Piece by Piece

*You faithfully answer our prayers with awesome deeds,
O God our savior. You are the hope of everyone on earth,
even those who sail on distant seas. You formed the mountains
by your power and armed yourself with mighty strength. You
quieted the raging oceans with their pounding waves and
silenced the shouting of the nations. Those who live at the
ends of the earth stand in awe of your wonders. From where
the sun rises to where it sets, you inspire shouts of joy.*
PSALM 65:5–8 NLT

The psalmist David wrote Psalm 65 while focusing on how awesome God is. David was so convinced of God's faithful work and mighty hands that he gave God the praise that He was due. Piece by piece God orchestrated all of creation. As David reflected in verse 9 (NLT), "You take care of the earth and water it, making it rich and fertile."

Think about it: God formed you. He created you!

Here's a little exercise for you today. Stand in front of the mirror and take a good look at yourself. Notice the delicate features of your face, your body, your hands, and your feet. Bit by bit, piece by piece, God made you. You are beautiful because you were created in His image (Genesis 1:27). He loves you! Praise Him for this body that He has formed.

*Jesus, I thank You for making me into the
woman I've become. I also thank You
for forming me into a mommy-to-be.*

Guided

*"You guided my conception and formed me in the womb.
You clothed me with skin and flesh, and you knit my bones
and sinews together. You gave me life and showed me
your unfailing love. My life was preserved by your care."*
JOB 10:10–12 NLT

Job lost everything. Everything. He lost his wealth, his children, and his servants. This brought him to a place of complete brokenness. He didn't hide from God in the middle of his pain and deep anguish, though. Even in his great loss, Job chose to praise and depend on God.

How about you? You might be reading today's devotion with a heavy heart. A part of you feels torn, already weighed down by the complexities of pregnancy and motherhood. So much of you yearns for a child, but you've walked through great loss. Maybe you've lost a child. Maybe you didn't grow up in a safe family environment and you fear how that will affect your ability to be a mommy.

There's hope in Job's story. The hope is that even though Job lost everything, eventually God gave it all back to him and even more! God walked Job through a series of tests to refine him, to sanctify him. God was still with Job, guiding his life. God gave, took away, but then gave back even more.

---

*Father, thank You for guiding me in this pregnancy
and motherhood journey. I look forward to
seeing how You will guide me.*

Whole and Holy

*With your very own hands you formed me; now breathe
your wisdom over me so I can understand you. When they
see me waiting, expecting your Word, those who fear you
will take heart and be glad. I can see now, GOD, that your
decisions are right; your testing has taught me what's true
and right. Oh, love me—and right now!—hold me tight! just
the way you promised. Now comfort me so I can live, really
live; your revelation is the tune I dance to. Let the fast-
talking tricksters be exposed as frauds; they tried to sell me
a bill of goods, but I kept my mind fixed on your counsel.
Let those who fear you turn to me for evidence of your wise
guidance. And let me live whole and holy, soul and body,
so I can always walk with my head held high.*

PSALM 119:73–80 MSG

Veronica couldn't believe it. She was glowing and had a
twinkle in her eyes.

For four years, she and her husband had tried to conceive.
Each attempt brought the couple to their knees.

Finally Veronica got pregnant. The journey brought the
couple closer together. It also brought her closer to God in a
more intimate way than she ever would have thought possible.
In her heart she rejoiced, knowing that the journey was worth it.

---

*Lord, thank You for the holy act You did on
the cross so that I can be made whole in You.*

Christ in You

My dear children, for (you) I am again in the
pains of childbirth until Christ is formed in you.
GALATIANS 4:19 NIV

The apostle Paul wrote to the Christian community in Galatia because he was concerned about the idols in their lives. Before they put their faith in Jesus Christ, many in Galatia were putting their faith, hope, and trust in other people. In essence Paul was concerned about what they were focusing on and who they were really worshipping.

As a mommy-to-be, you will find that many distractions will come up throughout the day. You might find yourself restless, longing for time with the Lord. You might feel a sense of guilt for being pulled in several different directions, and not always able to give 100 percent of yourself to every person or commitment.

Then comes the all-consuming message of God's grace, which is what the apostle Paul loved talking about. With Jesus Christ you have the daily opportunity to tap into His grace. Remember as a mommy-to-be that the most important thing you get done in the day isn't the laundry, the dishes, or your list of errands. Although those are important, the most crucial is spending time with God and His Word. Out of His fountain of grace, people—including your children—will get to experience the overflow of Christ in you!

Lord, it isn't easy being a mommy-to-be. Sometimes, like childbirth, it can be laborious. Mold me into Your image.

Mysterious Maker

*Just as you'll never understand the mystery of
life forming in a pregnant woman, so you'll never
understand the mystery at work in all that God does.*
ECCLESIASTES 11:5 MSG

In the book of Ecclesiastes, Solomon writes about the nuances and complexities of human existence. He writes about the beauty and tragedy that can come with witnessing the imperfections of life here on earth.

Even though medical evidence informs how God created a baby inside of your womb, it's still considered a great mystery. While you took a step of faith and did your part to create this new life, it's still amazing how God chose to orchestrate forming a baby inside of you. It's a miracle!

As Solomon reflects on this aspect of God, a mysterious maker, take a moment to reflect on all that God has done in your life. Think about all that He has already done for this baby and all that He will do in their life. Take some time today to pray for this baby's growth inside of you; all of their delicate, intricate parts.

---

*Lord, I pray for this baby, Your child that You are entrusting me
with, for however many days You have ordained for their life
here on earth. You have created this baby inside of me. I pray
for their growth and development inside of my womb. Please
help me to celebrate this child the way You desire. Despite my
imperfections, help me meet this baby's needs.*

The Craftsman

*The God Who produced and formed the world and all
things in it, being Lord of heaven and earth, does not
dwell in handmade shrines. Neither is He served by human
hands, as though He lacked anything, for it is He Himself
Who gives life and breath and all things to all (people).*
ACTS 17:24–25 AMPC

The apostle Paul was deeply troubled by the idols he saw
throughout the city of Athens. These idols took away the worship that God had in mind. Paul communicated a message of
grace, love, and mercy to those in the city to turn their focus
to the one, true God.

As a mommy-to-be, you're amazed thinking about all of the
detailed work that goes into having a baby. You might realize
just how amazing and intricate God is now that He's forming
a human being inside of you! There truly is so much that has
to happen inside of your body, and the baby's, in order to make
life a reality. This is something that God has had in mind since
creation. No one else can take the credit for creating this baby.

Consider the work God is doing inside of your womb. Meditate on Isaiah 64:8 (NLT), which says, "And yet, O LORD, you are
our Father. We are the clay, and you are the potter. We all are
formed by your hand."

---

*Father, I thank You that this baby and I are
fearfully and wonderfully crafted by You!*

Call to Me

"Thus says the LORD who made it, the LORD who formed it to establish it (the LORD is His name): 'Call to Me, and I will answer you, and show you great and mighty things, which you do not know.' "
JEREMIAH 33:2–3 NKJV

Isabella was so excited. She got pregnant on the first try. She couldn't believe how quickly it happened for her.

On the other hand, Isabella was also a bit shocked. She and her husband were only four months married and he was in his last year of graduate school. She was working full-time to make ends meet. But here she was, five weeks pregnant. The baby would arrive shortly after her husband finished his schooling.

As Isabella sat down to think about the situation, she noticed the Bible her husband left open on the coffee table from the night before. She picked it up and opened right to Jeremiah 33:2–3. As she read it she cried out to God.

"Jesus, I'm excited. I've dreamed of this day since I was a little girl. But here we are living in a 600-square-foot apartment. In this moment I choose to ask You to show me great and mighty things. Help me to believe You know all of our needs."

Lord, no matter what my situation may be with this pregnancy, I believe that You formed me and this baby. I believe that You know all of my needs. Help me to trust You each step of the way.

WEEK 6

♡

Knitted

Your baby is starting to show signs of
being knitted together. For example,
your baby's mouth, nose, and ears
are starting to develop. You might
start to feel the effects of morning
sickness and fatigue.

Divine Details

For You did form my inward parts; You did knit me together in my mother's womb. I will confess and praise You for You are fearful and wonderful and for the awful wonder of my birth! Wonderful are Your works, and that my inner self knows right well. My frame was not hidden from You when I was being formed in secret (and) intricately and curiously wrought (as if embroidered with various colors) in the depths of the earth (a region of darkness and mystery).
PSALM 139:13–15 AMPC

To be knitted is to become closely and firmly joined together, to grow together, as broken bones do. Things that are knitted together are closely and intimately united.

The psalmist understood that God knew him—every thought, every action, every single detail of his life.

Because you are a child, a daughter, of Jesus Christ, God knows everything about you! "Indeed, the very hairs of your head are all numbered. Don't be afraid; you are worth more than many sparrows" (Luke 12:7 NIV). The God who knitted you together inside of your mother's womb knows and loves you. This is true for the baby inside of you too!

Jesus, You are the Creator and Sustainer of life. This life is only by Your grace and miraculous work. I praise You for how You divinely detailed my life to connect with the life You are knitting together inside of me.

Become One

*That is why a man leaves his father and mother and
is united to his wife, and they become one flesh.*
GENESIS 2:24 NIV

In the beginning, God created man. From man He created woman. It was God's intimate design to use one man and one woman to create life.

From the beginning, God had it in mind to unite man and woman. It's a great mystery how two completely different people, male and female, can become one flesh. But through conception, pregnancy, and birth, we see a glimpse of God's intention for two bodies to be united and become one body.

It's also evident that God wanted humans to carry on the legacy of reproducing. Birth plays an intricate role in allowing for human existence to continue.

You are playing a big part in God's unique design and intention for the human race to carry on. As you united to become one flesh, God used that to start knitting together a new life. This new life will one day have an opportunity to come to know how much God loves them. Your child will have the chance to accept God into their life, give Him glory, and live out their calling.

---

*Father, thank You for knitting me together. Thank You for
this precious baby inside of me that You are knitting
together. Give me Your eyes to see just how awesome
Your works are in my life and in the life of this child.*

Strong Ties

I want them to be encouraged and knit together by strong ties of love. I want them to have complete confidence that they understand God's mysterious plan, which is Christ himself. In him lie hidden all the treasures of wisdom and knowledge.

COLOSSIANS 2:2–3 NLT

Jamie was feeling quite hesitant about the news. She wasn't as excited as some of her other friends were when they found out they were pregnant. *Is something wrong with me, God?* she thought. *Why do I not feel excited about this news that seems to make so many women happy?*

Jamie grew up in a challenging home. Her parents divorced when she was young. While her parents did the best they could, she still remembered division, chaos, and strife in the home. All she wanted as a child was some stability from her parents. As a teenager, she came to know Christ through youth group. It was there that Jamie learned that Jesus was the stabilizer in her life.

Paul shared good news with the believers in Colosse. When you are in Christ, you have a strong connection to the Father. You have access to all of the wisdom and knowledge you'll ever need as a mom, right at your fingertips.

Lord, I'm scared and excited about being a mommy. In the moments when I waver, help me to remember the strong ties I have in You! Help me to hold on to Your Word tightly. Thank You for loving me.

Double Up

Jamie shared her feelings with her husband. "Jeff, I thought I'd
be happy. Excited about the news that we're pregnant. But
I'm not. I feel scared. Terrified."

Jeff did his best to listen to Jamie. He wasn't afraid to tell
her the truth. "Are you afraid that you might repeat history,
Jamie? No matter how bad things could get between us, we
will seek wise counsel. We are a team, Jamie. I love you, and
I'm excited for our little family."

Jamie appreciated Jeff's insight and support. His words
helped her to realize why she was afraid. But her fears weren't
even reality.

If you are feeling any concerns or fears, know that you
are not alone. Jesus wants to provide you with an abundance
of wisdom and counsel. Take some time today to share your
worries with God about being pregnant. He's on your side,
partnering with you in the calling of motherhood.

---

*Lord, help me to share with You my feelings about this
pregnancy. Help me to cast all of my cares upon You. Help
me not to hold on to the pain of my past. Help me to double
up with You and be the best team possible for this baby.*

God's Gracious Gift

*Boaz married Ruth. She became his wife. Boaz slept
with her. By GOD's gracious gift she conceived and had
a son. The town women said to Naomi, "Blessed be GOD!
He didn't leave you without family to carry on your life.
May this baby grow up to be famous in Israel! He'll make
you young again! He'll take care of you in old age. And
this daughter-in-law who has brought him into the world
and loves you so much, why, she's worth more to you than
seven sons!" Naomi took the baby and held him in her arms,
cuddling him, cooing over him, waiting on him hand and
foot. The neighborhood women started calling him "Naomi's
baby boy!" But his real name was Obed. Obed was the
father of Jesse, and Jesse the father of David.*
RUTH 4:13–17 MSG

Jamie took some time with the Lord. She set aside a Saturday
afternoon to pray, journal, and read her Bible.

During that time, Jamie poured out her thoughts and feelings about pregnancy and motherhood to God. She wept over
some of the fears she had, as well as some of the pain she'd
experienced as a child. Jamie asked God for the strength not
to repeat history with this child. She resolved to lean into God's
grace and mercy for this baby's life.

---

*Jesus, this baby is a gift from You! Even when
I forget to ask You, I need Your mercy and
grace to raise this child of Yours well.*

Nourished and Knit Together

(Hold) fast to the Head, from whom all the body,
nourished and knit together by joints and ligaments,
grows with the increase that is from God.
COLOSSIANS 2:19 NKJV

"You are the source of life," Jamie prayed out loud to God. "You created me, and this baby inside of me, You also created. I pray over every cell. I pray over every extremity and organ. Knit this baby together. Help this baby get the nourishment it needs from my body during this pregnancy."

As Jamie sat on the park bench, she paused to gaze out toward the park. She could see and hear children giggling as they swung and slid down the slides. It caused her to think back to some of her good childhood memories. Like playing in the park or outside during recess.

"Lord, thank You for the good childhood memories that I do have. Not all of my childhood was bad. Thank You for using youth group to lead me to You. That was Your grace abounding in my life. I pray for this child. That they will come to know You as the One who nourished and knit them together inside of me."

God, being a mommy-to-be is a big calling. Please meet me where I'm at in this journey. Help me to remember the good times from my childhood. And help me to lean into Your grace and mercy to improve upon the shortcomings.

Unite My Heart

Teach me thy way, O Lord; I will walk in thy truth:
unite my heart to fear thy name.
PSALM 86:11 KJV

Jamie continued to reflect on the good in her childhood. Like how even though her parents divorced, they both came to accept Christ. In fact, her parents were regular church attenders. Jamie was also thankful that she still had a decent relationship with her mom and dad, despite the separation. Her parents had even reconciled and asked the kids for forgiveness.

Jamie thought about that for a moment. She was so thankful to have parents who were believers, who confessed their shortcomings and had the humility to ask their kids for forgiveness. She had always wished and prayed her parents would somehow get back together. But they both remained single.

Jamie picked up her Bible. Her reading plan for the day included Psalm 86, a prayer written by David. She read through it and stopped at verse 11. The Word became alive and active, and Psalm 86 resonated with her.

Take some time today to recount the trials in your life and how God has knitted them together for good (Romans 8:28).

Lord, You are worthy of my praise! Thank You for teaching me about You through the good and the bad in this life. Help me to focus on Your goodness despite my sinful ways. Help me to come to terms with my past, knowing You have knitted everything together for my good.

WEEK 7

♡

Embraced

Your baby is starting to develop extremities that resemble hands and feet, which one day will be used to hold on to you! You are continuing to experience the early onset of pregnancy, which may include food aversions, fatigue, cravings, and/or morning sickness.

Welcome

*These all died in faith, not having received the promises,
but having seen them afar off, and were persuaded of
them, and embraced them, and confessed that they
were strangers and pilgrims on the earth.*
HEBREWS 11:13 KJV

The King James Version of Hebrews 11:13 uses the word *embraced*, whereas the NIV and the NLT use the word *welcomed*.

To embrace someone is to clasp them in your arms and hug them, to gladly receive and willingly accept them. And when we welcome someone, we receive them with pleasure.

Over the next few weeks, months, and years, your life will be forever changed by this tiny baby inside of you. This child will affect every aspect of your body, your relationships, and how you make decisions for the future.

Hebrews 11 is often considered the Hall of Faith. The individuals written about in this chapter all did noble things for God. Some didn't even get to see their promise fulfilled on this side of heaven. Others watched as their lives were drastically changed as a result of their steps of faith. They welcomed and embraced all God had for them, even if it was uncomfortable.

---

*Lord, I desire to welcome and embrace this baby as a
gift from You. I thank You for all of the uncomfortable
changes ahead because I believe, by faith, that
they will strengthen my relationship with You.*

Believe

*It was by faith that even Sarah was able to have a child,
though she was barren and was too old. She believed that
God would keep his promise. And so a whole nation came
from this one man who was as good as dead—a nation with
so many people that, like the stars in the sky and the sand
on the seashore, there is no way to count them.*
HEBREWS 11:11–12 NLT

Abraham and Sarah embraced what God had for them. Even
when they tried to take matters into their own hands, God was
still gracious.

Sarah said to Abraham in Genesis 16:2 (NIV), "The LORD has
kept me from having children. Go, sleep with my slave; perhaps I can build a family through her." Sarah's slave, Hagar,
bore them a child.

Genesis 15:4–6 (NIV) says: "Then the word of the LORD came
to him (Abraham): 'This man will not be your heir, but a son
who is your own flesh and blood will be your heir.' He took him
outside and said, 'Look up at the sky and count the stars—if
indeed you can count them.' Then he said to him, 'So shall
your offspring be.' Abram believed the LORD, and he credited
it to him as righteousness."

Abraham was one hundred years old when he and Sarah
bore their own flesh and blood, Isaac.

---

*Lord, thank You for this baby.
I embrace the promise You have given me.*

From Lost to Blessed

"You're blessed when you feel you've lost what is most dear to you. Only then can you be embraced by the One most dear to you. You're blessed when you're content with just who you are—no more, no less. That's the moment you find yourselves proud owners of everything that can't be bought."
MATTHEW 5:4–5 MSG

During His Sermon on the Mount, Jesus taught His disciples about some of the most important moral principles of the faith. With each truth came a blessing.

These principles apply to many aspects of life, including motherhood. Being a mom means that you embrace a calling, as well as a responsibility, to raise a child and live out your faith. This calling will require you to extend grace and mercy, on a regular basis, to your child and to yourself. A lot is at stake, but there are also many blessings!

What's the biggest blessing of all as you embrace this calling? The coos, the smiles, and the laughter of a baby are priceless. But the most precious blessing is to know that as you serve a child whom He loves unconditionally, you are being fully embraced by your heavenly Father.

Lord, with the changes that are already taking place inside and outside of my body, I'm losing a part of myself. Yet I thank You because I'm gaining even more of Your presence as I embrace being a mommy-to-be.

Love and Compassion

"So he returned home to his father. And while he was still a long way off, his father saw him coming. Filled with love and compassion, he ran to his son, embraced him, and kissed him."
LUKE 15:20 NLT

Lost but not forgotten. That's how one father felt about one of his sons. As Jesus shared the parable of the lost son, he used it as an illustration of how a child of God may go astray, perhaps rebel, for some time. But God, in His great love and compassion, will always welcome that one lost child home with a full embrace. As a mom, you'd do the same.

Maybe you have felt the tug of this world. Perhaps there is a sin that still brings shame into your life. Maybe there's a choice you made that wasn't the right one. Now is an opportunity, wherever you're at, to embrace Jesus the way that He wants to embrace you.

Take some time to talk out loud to God. Confess the things that weigh heavily on your heart. Ask God for forgiveness, and receive His mercy and grace. He loves you. No sin is too big for Him to forgive.

Jesus, I come before You in need of Your healing touch. I'm sorry for the choices I've made that have gone against Your will. In the areas of my life where I'm lost as a mommy-to-be, I need for You to embrace me where I'm at in this journey.

My Own

He had told Rachel that he was a relative of her father and a son of Rebekah. So she ran and told her father. As soon as Laban heard the news about Jacob, his sister's son, he hurried to meet him. He embraced him and kissed him and brought him to his home, and there Jacob told him all these things. Then Laban said to him, "You are my own flesh and blood."
GENESIS 29:12–14 NIV

Amy found out that she was pregnant for the third time. She adored the idea of having a third baby in the house. She knew it was a desire God put on her heart. But Amy also felt challenged by not having the kind of help she needed from her family of origin, and even extended family members.

But then Amy was reminded of her friends, the women from church, and the community she came to know through a local moms' group.

A mentor once said to Amy that even though her own flesh and blood might reject her, God had adopted her as His daughter! Amy could consider herself God's very own flesh and blood!

When Amy remembered these wise words, she chose to believe by faith that God was embracing her.

God, when I feel overwhelmed by the thought of embracing and taking care of my own flesh and blood, help me to remember that You know our needs before I even ask. Thank You for adopting me into Your family.

The Appointed Time

So he said, "What then is to be done for her?" And Gehazi answered, "Actually, she has no son, and her husband is old." So he said, "Call her." When he had called her, she stood in the doorway. Then he said, "About this time next year you shall embrace a son." And she said, "No, my lord. Man of God, do not lie to your maidservant!" But the woman conceived, and bore a son when the appointed time had come, of which Elisha had told her.

2 KINGS 4:14–17 NKJV

Have you ever received something but just couldn't believe it? Think back to how you felt. Was there joy, shock, disbelief? Did you feel like you deserved it?

Imagine how the Shunammite woman must have felt when Elisha told her she would embrace a son. Would you have questioned what Elisha said?

A year later you come to realize that what Elisha, this man of God, said to you was completely accurate. You conceived and bore a son.

If you've been waiting to be pregnant for the first, second, third time or more, this is a special time for you! It's an appointed time. Years from now you'll look back on this time in awe of what God was doing in and through your body.

Jesus, the older I get, please help me not to forget how special this time is as I carry this baby inside of my womb.

Embracing a Miracle

He called Gehazi and said, "Get the Shunammite woman in
here!" He called her and she came in. Elisha said, "Embrace
your son!" She fell at Elisha's feet, face to the ground in reverent
awe. Then she embraced her son and went out with him.
2 KINGS 4:36–37 MSG

A child was promised to the Shunammite woman, and so it came to pass. She conceived and bore a son, just like Elisha said she would. A son she dearly loved and embraced.

Then, one day, the unexpected happened. The boy wasn't feeling well. The woman laid him on her lap and he died. She asked for Elisha's help. Elisha came and prayed and prayed over this boy. And then a miracle occurred. The boy woke up—he was alive!

Being a mommy-to-be can be a journey filled with many ups and downs. One doctor's appointment might raise some concerns. Another one might go really well. One day you might feel extremely fatigued, or maybe almost paralyzed by round ligament pain. Other days you might feel great and like you want to tackle your to-do list.

Part of embracing the miracle going on inside of your belly is to trust God with the promise He has placed within you. The promise of new life.

Father, in the days and weeks ahead, help me to
embrace this baby inside of my belly. Just as You
gave the Shunammite woman a child, thank
You for giving me this little miracle.

WEEK 8

♡

Accepted

♡

Your baby continues to develop.
Meanwhile, as you accept this new
calling, you'll be getting ready
for your first prenatal doctor
appointment and tests.

Admired and Approved

Esther was the daughter of Abihail, who was Mordecai's
uncle. (Mordecai had adopted his younger cousin Esther.)
When it was Esther's turn to go to the king, she accepted
the advice of Hegai, the eunuch in charge of the harem.
She asked for nothing except what he suggested,
and she was admired by everyone who saw her.
ESTHER 2:15 NLT

When you accept something, you receive it with approval or favor, and sometimes you undertake responsibilities, duties, and honors along with it.

Esther was a woman in the Bible who wanted to be admired and approved for noble reasons. She was a queen, but if Esther revealed her nationality and family background, she might have been mistreated. She stayed faithful in the position God put her in, and at the right time she revealed her background. Esther was accepted based upon her faithfulness to God in the position to which He appointed her. Her acceptance wasn't based on family upbringing or nationality; it was based on her identity as a daughter of God.

When you were conceived, you were accepted by God. In fact, before you were even thought of, you were loved by God (Jeremiah 1:5). Perhaps you have felt the sting of rejection in this world because of your past. Take heart—God loves you!

Jesus, thank You for accepting me just as I am.
Set me apart to do noble things for You as a mommy-to-be.

Mommy Mistakes

God spoke to Moses: "When a calf or lamb or goat is born,
it is to stay with its mother for seven days. After the eighth
day, it is acceptable as an offering, a gift to God. Don't
slaughter both a cow or ewe and its young on the same
day. When you sacrifice a Thanksgiving-Offering to God,
do it right so it will be acceptable. Eat it on the same day;
don't leave any leftovers until morning. I am God."
LEVITICUS 22:29–30 MSG

Leviticus is one of those books in the Bible that can be considered detailed and daunting. Conversely, this book in the Bible is holy, set apart, and filled with examples of worship. It is also a reminder of the way things used to be. Before Jesus died on the cross for the forgiveness of sins, God's followers had to follow the religious and ritualistic methods of sacrifice and offerings in order for sins to be forgiven.

This is awesome news to you as a mommy-to-be because what Jesus did can change your perspective. You are free to live and parent under God's abundant grace and mercy! You do not have to keep a record of your wrongs or perform sacrifices in order for sins to be forgiven.

Father, thank You that I no longer have to live under the
penalty of sin. Thank You for accepting me so that I can
have direct access to You when I make a mommy mistake.

Children of God

But to all who believed him and accepted him,
he gave the right to become children of God.
JOHN 1:12 NLT

Elizabeth grew up in a modest suburban neighborhood. Her family wasn't perfect, and as she got older the less they went to church. She was brought up with some appreciation for Jesus, and she knew some things about Him, but she didn't have a relationship with Him.

During college she met Andrea. Andrea was in several of her classes and they started studying together. Their shared time together grew into a unique friendship. One day Andrea shared about her faith. Elizabeth took interest and asked several questions. A few weeks later, around Easter, Elizabeth put her faith in Jesus and began a relationship with Him.

A few weeks after that, Elizabeth got baptized. She was given John 1:12–13 at her baptism as a reminder that she was a child of God. She began to pray about the mom she one day hoped to be. Andrea started to pray with Elizabeth for a future husband and future children. These times of prayer caused the two friends to reflect on what it meant to be a child of God, as well as one whom God would use to bring His children into the world.

Thank You, Jesus, for this body that You have
given me. Thank You for accepting me as
Your daughter and calling me to be a mom.

House of Prayer

All these I will bring to My holy mountain and make them joyful in My house of prayer. Their burnt offerings and their sacrifices will be accepted on My altar; for My house will be called a house of prayer for all peoples.
Isaiah 56:7 AMPC

During college, Elizabeth united with her friends from campus ministry to pray. They devoted twenty-four hours to constant prayer. They prayed in shifts for numerous things. One of the things Elizabeth prayed for was their future husbands and their future children.

Five years later, Elizabeth remembered those prayers. Here she was, eight weeks pregnant and getting ready to embark on a huge change. Her other friends from college who had prayed that day were also pregnant. Some with their first, others with their second or third child. Although many miles apart from each other, they decided once again to commit to pray for each other's husbands and children.

In this moment, take some time to reflect on those who have prayed for you over the years. Thank God for them and consider how you might be able to pray for them too.

Lord, thank You for the spiritual mentors who have gone before me and have come beside me to pray for me. I pray for them right now. Bless them in all that they do.

Soul Friends

By the time David had finished reporting to Saul, Jonathan was deeply impressed with David—an immediate bond was forged between them. He became totally committed to David. From that point on he would be David's number-one advocate and friend. Saul received David into his own household that day, no more to return to the home of his father.

1 SAMUEL 18:1–2 MSG

Through the commitment to pray for each other, Elizabeth and her friends from college became soul friends. While the years and miles between them created some distance, their bond was in the Lord. As their pregnancies became news to one another, they all rejoiced in the fruit of the seeds they had sown in prayer years prior.

They all celebrated with each other through social media. God was clearly doing an awesome work in their lives!

One friend in particular shared her fears and struggles with being pregnant for the second time. Her previous pregnancy resulted in a miscarriage. She was trusting God to provide a healthy baby. The friends committed to pray before she had to go in for her prenatal appointments.

Consider any of your friends and acquaintances who have become a mommy-to-be. Pray for them, but also ask them how you can be praying. You never know—you just might end up becoming soul friends!

Jesus, You are the Creator and Sustainer of life. Show me other moms I can be praying for as they walk the mommy-to-be journey.

Glory to God

Therefore receive one another, just as Christ
also received us, to the glory of God.
ROMANS 15:7 NKJV

Humans were created in the image of God (Genesis 1:27).
People were created not to bring glory to themselves, but
to glorify God (Isaiah 43:7). Being a mommy-to-be is a huge
opportunity to give glory, and bring glory, to the One who is
the Creator of life.

In this scripture, the apostle Paul wasn't just issuing a call to
action to glorify God on an individual level. Rather, Paul urged
the Romans to glorify God together.

As you accept the fact that you are pregnant, and believe
that God is the Creator of life, consider how you can give
God the glory throughout your pregnancy. Maybe it's praying
for those who will cross your path as you raise this child. Maybe
it's just praying for your baby as they form and develop inside
of your womb. Or pray for the doctors and medical staff who
will get to interact with you and this baby. If anyone asks, let
them know to be praying for you and your baby. Why? Because
where two or more gather in Jesus' name to pray, there He is
also (Matthew 18:20).

Lord, I give You the glory for creating the baby inside of me.
Help me to find ways to glorify You throughout this whole
mommy-to-be process. Give me the words to speak.

A God-Incident

*We accept human testimony, but God's
testimony is greater because it is the testimony
of God, which he has given about his Son.*
1 JOHN 5:9 NIV

Elizabeth knew that it was ordained by God for her to come to know Christ in college, meet several women to unite in prayer, and now come to learn that so many of them were expecting babies. She didn't consider this a coincidence and gave glory to God for blessing their lives.

God, in His goodness, has orchestrated events in your life that are a testament to Him and His faithfulness. Often we're tempted to think that somehow human efforts made something come to pass or that it was serendipitous. In all actuality, these God-incidents are what paved the way for some people to see God in the lives of others.

Take some time to pray today for those you will cross paths with throughout this pregnancy. As you accept all that lies ahead (even some of the details that you aren't expecting while expecting!), pray for the doctors and medical staff. Pray for a pediatrician. Pray for any classes you decide to take while pregnant: for the teachers and classmates. If you plan on breastfeeding, pray for the lactation consultant. You never know what divine appointments God might orchestrate in and through you.

Lord, help me to make the most of every opportunity and conversation while I'm a mommy-to-be. Help me to have eyes to see Your God-incidents and divine appointments.

WEEK 9

♡

Captivated

You may be captivated to know that, although still very small, your baby is starting to look more like a little person. You will probably continue to notice internal, and some external, changes physically and emotionally.

Holy Beauty

The same goes for you wives: Be good wives to your husbands, responsive to their needs. There are husbands who, indifferent as they are to any words about God, will be captivated by your life of holy beauty. What matters is not your outer appearance—the styling of your hair, the jewelry you wear, the cut of your clothes—but your inner disposition.

1 PETER 3:1–4 MSG

Peter was one of Jesus' twelve disciples. He had a strong faith in Jesus, but he had his imperfections too. God still used Peter to be a catalyst for the Gospel.

In 1 Peter 3, Peter expressed to husbands and wives his hopes for them in Christ. In verse 7 (MSG) he wrote, "The same goes for you husbands: Be good husbands to your wives. Honor them, delight in them. As women they lack some of your advantages. But in the new life of God's grace, you're equals. Treat your wives, then, as equals so your prayers don't run aground."

So why is inner beauty so captivating?

Because inner beauty is holy, set apart. As a mommy-to-be you have the chance to radiate God's beauty from the inside out.

Lord, as my body and hormones continue to change, help me to see the pregnancy process as captivating and beautiful.

Be You and Let Christ Through

*Let your light so shine before men that they may
see your moral excellence and your praiseworthy,
noble, and good deeds and recognize and honor
and praise and glorify your Father Who is in heaven.*
MATTHEW 5:16 AMPC

Anna was cleaning up her children's play area. At nine weeks pregnant she felt exhausted, but she kept putting off the chore. Her kids were out of the house so she knew she could take fifteen minutes to tidy things up, then take a nap.

Anna could tell already that this pregnancy was a lot different than her first two. The fatigue set in a lot sooner, and she was feeling nauseous. But on this day, although tired, she wasn't dealing with morning sickness as badly as the days before.

As she rummaged through her kids' stuff, she noticed that a teacher had written on her daughter Sophia's Sunday school coloring page: *Let your light shine. Be you and let Christ through.* Anna was captivated by the key verse, Matthew 5:16.

Being pregnant has its challenges, and it's tempting to give in to the raging hormones. But even in the middle of being who you are as a mommy-to-be, you can still be a light to the world around you.

*Jesus, help me to be a light to my children, neighbors,
acquaintances, family members, and friends. Even as I
walk through the ups and downs of this pregnancy,
may they see You flow through my character.*

Night-Lights

Your word is a lamp to my feet and a light to my path.
I have sworn and confirmed that I will keep Your
righteous judgments. I am afflicted very much;
Revive me, O LORD, according to Your word.
PSALM 119:105–107 NKJV

"Mommy, can you leave the night-light on?" Isabella asked her mom before nap time.

"Um, is everything okay, sweetheart? This is just nap time. It's not nighttime. Usually Daddy puts the night-light on for you in the evening."

"Yes, everything is okay. My Sunday school teacher said I can be a light to the world. That when I show kindness and love toward others, it's captivating. So beautiful that they will want to know more about Jesus."

"That's right, Bella! But if you stay up and stare at the night light for too long, you will get really tired and not take as good of a nap today," Mom said, trying to reason with her. At nine weeks pregnant all Mom wanted was her three-year-old daughter to take a good nap so she wouldn't be fussy for the rest of the day, and so that Mom could rest.

"But Mom! How will I know how beautiful the princess night-light is if I don't see it?" Isabella responded. "I don't want it to be hidden."

Lord, I need You to revive my mommy-to-be spirit.
Psalm 119:93 (NLT) is my prayer: "I will never forget
your commandments, for by them you give me life."

Let It Shine

*One thing have I asked of the Lord, that will I seek,
inquire for, and (insistently) require: that I may dwell in the
house of the Lord (in His presence) all the days of my life,
to behold and gaze upon the beauty (the sweet
attractiveness and the delightful loveliness) of the Lord
and to meditate, consider, and inquire in His temple.*
PSALM 27:4 AMPC

Isabella's mom decided to leave the night light on. As she walked out of her daughter's bedroom, she heard Isabella singing, "This little light of mine, I'm gonna let it shine. This little light of mine, I'm gonna let it shine. This little light of mine, I'm gonna let it shine. Let it shine, let it shine, let it shine."

A smile slowly started to appear on Mom's face and lit her up. She could tell her daughter's message resonated with her. In fact, Isabella's illustration captivated Mom so much that once she got downstairs, she picked up a Bible and sat down on the couch.

With her legs propped up on the coffee table, she began to read Psalm 27 and focused on verse 4. She prayed and asked God to fill their house. As they prepared for the arrival of this second child, she prayed for His light to shine in all of them as they embarked on this new transition.

---

*Lord, as I adjust to all of the changes that are already
taking place, please be my light and source of strength.*

Pregnancy Producing Power

For once you were full of darkness, but now you have light from the Lord. So live as people of light! For this light within you produces only what is good and right and true. Carefully determine what pleases the Lord.
EPHESIANS 5:8–10 NLT

There's something about pregnancy that transforms you from the inside out.

You notice it shortly after you get pregnant. Your body changes; your hormones change. Everything is changing! It's the grace of God that pregnancy takes forty weeks, plus or minus a few days, because it takes time for a mommy-to-be to prepare her heart, mind, soul, and home.

What the apostle Paul was pointing out in Ephesians 5 is the importance of imitating God. As you imitate God and live a life that is set apart, you become a light and bear much fruit.

Pregnancy and motherhood might cause you to let go of, or stop doing, some things that you did before you were pregnant. You might never want to eat certain foods again because you understand the health ramifications for your and your child's body. There might be songs or television shows you just don't want to listen to or watch, because you want what flows through your mind and house to be edifying.

In the long run you're actually being filled with a new measure of the power of the Holy Spirit!

Jesus, thank You for helping me to lay down my life.
I want more of Your presence and power.

Pregnancy Psalm

*Give to the LORD, O families of the peoples, give to the
LORD glory and strength. Give to the LORD the glory due
His name; bring an offering, and come before Him.
Oh, worship the LORD in the beauty of holiness!*
1 CHRONICLES 16:28–29 NKJV

David sang a song of praise to God. A song filled with thanks-giving, awe, and wonder for who God was in his life. A song that was captivated by His beauty and holiness.

Think back to when you found out you were pregnant. Were you excited or scared? How do you feel now?

Take some time to express your thoughts and feelings about this pregnancy to God. Like David who wrote a song of praise in 1 Chronicles 16:7–36, consider writing a pregnancy poem or song. It could be something you keep in a journal or in a baby scrapbook.

Here are some things to consider as you write:

- What are you thankful to God for?

- If your baby read this psalm ten years from now, what do you want them to know about? For example, perhaps there's a neat testimony that led up to you getting pregnant that you want them to know about.

- Write some words of prayer for this pregnancy.

- Write some hopes and dreams for this child of God.

---

*Father, You are worthy of my praise. Show me how to write a
psalm that honors and glorifies You during this pregnancy.*

Set Apart

*But when God, who set me apart from my mother's womb
and called me by his grace, was pleased to reveal his Son
in me so that I might preach him among the Gentiles, my
immediate response was not to consult any human being.*
GALATIANS 1:15–16 NIV

The apostle Paul lived a different lifestyle before he fully committed himself to Jesus Christ.

In Galatians 1:11–12 (NIV) Paul wrote to Christians in Galatia: "I want you to know, brothers and sisters, that the gospel I preached is not of human origin. I did not receive it from any man, nor was I taught it; rather, I received it by revelation from Jesus Christ."

Paul recounted his previous way of life because he was captivated by what God had done in and through him. Captivated to the point that he had to tell people about how God called him into ministry. God set Paul apart for a divine purpose.

The baby inside of you will one day be presented with the opportunity to consider living for Christ. Take some time to pray for your baby and for the day that they come to hear about the saving message of God's grace, mercy, and forgiveness.

---

*Dear Jesus, thank You for dying on the cross for the
forgiveness of my sins. I pray that this baby inside
of me will one day hear the Gospel message,
be captivated by You, and receive You into their life.*

WEEK 10

Called

This early in the pregnancy, your baby's organs and structures are now in place. You might continue to feel fatigued, and you might start noticing a small baby bump.

Lean on God

A third time the Lord called, "Samuel!" And Samuel got up and went to Eli and said, "Here I am; you called me." Then Eli realized that the Lord was calling the boy. So Eli told Samuel, "Go and lie down, and if he calls you, say, 'Speak, Lord, for your servant is listening.'" So Samuel went and lay down in his place. The Lord came and stood there, calling as at the other times, "Samuel! Samuel!" Then Samuel said, "Speak, for your servant is listening." And the Lord said to Samuel: "See, I am about to do something in Israel that will make the ears of everyone who hears about it tingle."

1 Samuel 3:8–11 niv

Samuel thought Eli was calling him. It took three times for them to realize it was God.

How many times have you been hesitant to respond to God's calling? Being a mommy-to-be is a calling and a great responsibility. You might feel inadequate, unqualified, and fearful about what lies ahead over the next several weeks.

Samuel understood this because 1 Samuel 3:1 (niv) says, "The boy Samuel ministered before the Lord under Eli. In those days the word of the Lord was rare; there were not many visions."

Samuel didn't have a lot to rely on. You might not have a lot to rely on either. But Samuel had God's calling on his life, and so do you.

Lord, help me to accept this mommy-to-be calling on my life. Help me to lean on You.

One Little Child

*And He called a little child to Himself and put him in
the midst of them, and said, Truly I say to you, unless
you repent (change, turn about) and become like little
children (trusting, lowly, loving, forgiving), you can never
enter the kingdom of heaven (at all). Whoever will humble
himself therefore and become like this little child (trusting,
lowly, loving, forgiving) is greatest in the kingdom of heaven.
And whoever receives and accepts and welcomes one little
child like this for My sake and in My name receives
and accepts and welcomes Me.*
MATTHEW 18:2–5 AMPC

One of Jesus' disciples asked, "Who is the greatest in the kingdom of heaven?"

Jesus' response was beautiful. Breathtaking. A high calling
to those who want to follow Him, and to those who want to be
received by Him.

Matthew 18:10 (NLT) says, "Beware that you don't look down
on any of these little ones. For I tell you that in heaven their
angels are always in the presence of my heavenly Father."

Children are a gift and a reward from the Lord (Psalm
127:3). So consider it a very high calling that you are pregnant.
It is not something to look down upon. Rather it is something
to be praised.

*Lord, thank You for this little one inside of me.
Even though I feel tired and weary because of this
calling, I trust that many blessings will result from this birth.*

Called to Serve

We have been rescued from our enemies so we can serve God without fear, in holiness and righteousness for as long as we live. "And you, my little son, will be called the prophet of the Most High, because you will prepare the way for the Lord. You will tell his people how to find salvation through forgiveness of their sins.

LUKE 1:74–77 NLT

John's father, Zechariah, was filled with the Holy Spirit. As a result, he prophesied that John was called by God to be a prophet. A person who would prepare the way for Jesus Christ.

To be a prophet and make a way for Jesus was a very high calling, a position of humility and honor. It was also a call to obedient service and sacrifice for God's kingdom work.

The same is true as a mommy-to-be. Your role is a very high calling. It requires a lot of your time, energy, effort, money, and other resources. It's a huge honor but also a sacrifice. It asks you to serve your family, even when it's hard and when you don't feel like it.

And consider Jesus. He had a high calling on His life too. It required a lot of service and sacrifice, and it cost Him His life. But in the end, God resurrected Him to new life!

Lord, I thank You for calling me to serve this baby. Help me to have Your perspective when the days are long.

An Announcement

And the angel answered and said to her, "The Holy Spirit will come upon you, and the power of the Highest will overshadow you; therefore, also, that Holy One who is to be born will be called the Son of God. Now indeed, Elizabeth your relative has also conceived a son in her old age; and this is now the sixth month for her who was called barren. For with God nothing will be impossible."

LUKE 1:35–37 NKJV

The news was inconceivable. For nearly five years, Faith and Danny had tried to have kids. They went to great lengths in prayer, counseling, and doctor consultations. Nothing seemed to work. At times they doubted, questioned, wondered if it was ever going to happen.

They decided to adopt a child. Two months after they brought their son home from the hospital, Faith had some amazing news.

After not getting her monthly menstrual cycle, she picked up a pregnancy test. After much shock, she shouted from their upstairs bathroom, "I'm pregnant!"

The couple thought they were never going to have kids naturally. But God had other plans for their young, growing family.

Whatever obstacles you have faced leading up to accepting the mommy-to-be calling, praise God for what He has made possible in and through you!

Jesus, thank You for this divine masterpiece You are orchestrating inside of me. Help me never to forget that You are the God of the possible.

Called by Name

God knew what he was doing from the very beginning. He decided from the outset to shape the lives of those who love him along the same lines as the life of his Son. The Son stands first in the line of humanity he restored. We see the original and intended shape of our lives there in him. After God made that decision of what his children should be like, he followed it up by calling people by name. After he called them by name, he set them on a solid basis with himself. And then, after getting them established, he stayed with them to the end, gloriously completing what he had begun.
ROMANS 8:29–30 MSG

The apostle Paul wanted the Romans to understand what it meant to live a life fully yielded to Christ. Further along in the text, Paul wrote that God wanted His people to have a name—because a name bears purpose.

Have you taken the time to understand the meaning of your name? Take some time to research the meanings of your first, middle, and even last names. Reflect on how you have lived out your name, your calling.

God has a name in mind for your baby too. Start praying about what it needs to be.

Jesus, You gave me a name. I'm mirroring the image of You. This child inside of me also mirrors Your image. In the days and weeks ahead, please lead me to the right name for this child.

Follow the Leader

For God called you to do good, even if it means
suffering, just as Christ suffered for you. He is your
example, and you must follow in his steps.
1 PETER 2:21 NLT

At a young age Christina was involved with youth group. She loved her friends from church. She accepted Christ in elementary school. But in high school, her mom became very sick. During Christina's senior year, her mom passed away.

Shortly after Christina's mom passed away, a friend's mom mentored her during those last few months before she went off to college.

Christina received the guidance well, but during college she started to live a different life. She didn't get very involved with a campus ministry. She made it through school but developed some unhealthy habits. Two years after college she found herself in a relationship and soon discovered she was pregnant.

In that moment Christina wanted to cry, and missed her mom. She prayed for the first time in a long time. She reached out to the mom who had mentored her during her senior year. They got together for lunch, and Christina shared the news. The mentor decided she would commit to meeting with Christina regularly for Bible study and prayer and helped Christina rededicate her life to Christ.

Lord, as a mommy-to-be, I haven't always made the best
choices. Help me to turn away from unhealthy behaviors
so that I can follow You while parenting this baby.

That's Mine!

But now (in spite of past judgments for Israel's sins), thus says the Lord, He Who created you, O Jacob, and He Who formed you, O Israel: Fear not, for I have redeemed you (ransomed you by paying a price instead of leaving you captives); I have called you by your name; you are Mine.

ISAIAH 43:1 AMPC

What started out as a good idea, to get her two oldest boys to play together so Jennifer could sit on the couch for a few minutes, blew up like a giant balloon and popped before she could even say one of their names.

"Joseph Elijah and Thomas James, stop it right now!" Jennifer exclaimed.

At ten weeks pregnant, she felt tears starting to stream down her face.

"Boys, Mommy is restless. I just need some time to rest. Can you please play together nicely?"

"Sorry, Mom." Joseph, who was the oldest, led in apologizing.

"I'm sorry too, Mom," Thomas added.

"Mom, what's that in your hand?" Joseph asked.

"Oh, this is my Bible. I'm reading Isaiah 43 today."

"Can you read it to us?" Thomas asked.

It wasn't what Mom had in mind, but she led the boys into the family room. They all snuggled on the couch. They discussed how fighting over the blocks was frivolous compared to who they are in Christ.

Lord, as a mommy-to-be I can feel so restless one minute and relaxed the next. Help me to receive the most important truth: I am Yours and You are mine!

WEEK 11

♡

Comprehend

Your baby will soon be able to
open and close their hands. As the
first trimester is nearing the finish
line, you might still feel tired or deal
with morning sickness. Or you might
start to notice improvements in
how you are feeling.

A Masterpiece

For we are God's (own) handiwork (His workmanship),
recreated in Christ Jesus, (born anew) that we may do those
good works which God predestined (planned beforehand)
for us (taking paths which He prepared ahead of time),
that we should walk in them (living the good life which He
prearranged and made ready for us to live).
EPHESIANS 2:10 AMPC

Elisha wasn't feeling well. She picked up her phone and called her OBGYN's office.

"I think I need to come in. I'm not feeling good. I've had some cramping this morning. I don't remember having this in the beginning of my other pregnancies," she told the receptionist.

Elisha was able to make an appointment and got in right away to see her OB. After a full examination, the doctor did an ultrasound to make sure everything looked okay on the inside.

This was Elisha's third pregnancy, and the earliest ultrasound she'd ever gotten. It was mesmerizing to see the little baby's heart beating and the movement of the baby's hands.

"Wow, this truly is amazing to see my baby this early on in my pregnancy. Such a gift from God," Elisha commented.

After the ultrasound, the doctor shared the results. Everything was okay, but Elisha was ordered to rest.

"I'll see you next week," the OB reminded her. "And yes, a baby is a gift from God. Here are some ultrasound pictures for you to take home."

Father, I can't comprehend the masterpiece
You are creating inside of me!

Scratching the Surface

"Fear not, for I am with you; I will bring your descendants from the east, and gather you from the west; I will say to the north, 'Give them up!' And to the south, 'Do not keep them back!' Bring My sons from afar, and My daughters from the ends of the earth—everyone who is called by My name, whom I have created for My glory; I have formed him, yes, I have made him."
Isaiah 43:5–7 NKJV

It's difficult to comprehend the breadth of God's love. Isaiah was a prophet. He shared a message about God's love, grace, mercy, and favor for the nation of Israel. He also communicated this same message to each person who comprised the nation of Israel.

Every life, every breath, mattered to God back then. Every life, every breath, matters to God today.

You and your baby might be two of many, many people in the world. As far as the east is from the west, God loves everyone! It's hard to fully grasp this with our human minds, but being a mommy-to-be might help to scratch the surface of God's love and compassion for all of humankind.

Lord, I'm not You, so it's hard for me to grasp how high, wide, and deep Your love is for me and this tiny baby. Show me what this love is like so that I can somehow extend it to my child. For Your glory.

Sherbet in the Sky

When I applied my mind to know wisdom and to observe the labor that is done on earth—people getting no sleep day or night—then I saw all that God has done. No one can comprehend what goes on under the sun. Despite all their efforts to search it out, no one can discover its meaning. Even if the wise claim they know, they cannot really comprehend it.

ECCLESIASTES 8:16–17 NIV

"Mommy, today was such a great day!" Bridget exclaimed.

At eleven weeks pregnant, Maria appreciated her daughter's enthusiasm as they got ready for bed. "I love how it's getting warmer outside. And I love how I got to ride my bike today. And I love how the sunset was just so beautiful!"

"What colors did you see in the sunset tonight?" Mom asked.

"Pink, red, orange! It reminded me of eating sherbet! Yum! Can we get some of that at the grocery store this weekend, Mom?"

"Sure. We can get some," Mom replied while helping Bridget get her pajamas on.

"Mom, did God make the colors in the sky tonight?"

"I believe so."

"You know how I think He made them, Mom?"

"How?"

"I think He took sherbet and painted the sky with it!"

"That's a good guess! I can't comprehend how, but I believe He does something extraordinary in order to make those colors."

Lord, thank You for creating beauty in this world—in my mommy-to-be belly, in my children, in what I see.

Brought to Life

So, my very dear friends, don't get thrown off course. Every desirable and beneficial gift comes out of heaven. The gifts are rivers of light cascading down from the Father of Light. There is nothing deceitful in God, nothing two-faced, nothing fickle. He brought us to life using the true Word, showing us off as the crown of all his creatures.

JAMES 1:16–18 MSG

First-century Jewish Christians were scattered among the nations. James encouraged them to live a life that accepted, even anticipated, that there would be trials and tribulations. Being a believer of Jesus meant there would be suffering.

James also reminded believers that it was a joy and a blessing to endure times of testing and pressure-filled situations. During those seasons, believers would experience the abundant life that is only found in Christ.

As a pregnant mom, you will face trials and testing. There will be moments when you feel like you have poured out everything—physically, emotionally, and spiritually—to your family.

Just before you give birth, you might even feel out of control. A sense of losing yourself.

Through birth, you are brought back to life. You labor to bring new life into this world. It's hard to comprehend, but in delivery you die to self and start the process of a new life with your child.

Lord, thank You for dying on the cross so that I can experience Your resurrection power in my life.

So Big!

Oh, how great are God's riches and wisdom and knowledge! How impossible it is for us to understand his decisions and his ways! For who can know the LORD's thoughts? Who knows enough to give him advice? And who has given him so much that he needs to pay it back? For everything comes from him and exists by his power and is intended for his glory. All glory to him forever! Amen.
ROMANS 11:33–36 NLT

Amanda was exhausted, and she was still dealing with food aversions. She called one of the moms' group leaders from church to let her know she and her son wouldn't be at the playdate.

"I'm sorry, Tess, but we're not going to make it."

"Not a problem, Amanda. We totally understand! We'll be praying for you!"

Amanda prayed that Zachary wouldn't throw a fit because they weren't going to the indoor adventure park. *God, give me wisdom for how to share this with Zach. I'm so tired. I don't have the strength to deal with a temper tantrum.*

Zachary came into the family room and overheard his mom's prayer.

"Mommy, are you talking to God?"

"Yes, buddy. It's just that. . .we're not going to the indoor playground today. I was praying that you would be okay with that. Mommy doesn't feel well and—"

"It's okay, Mommy! God is so much bigger. Can we pray together instead?"

Lord, thank You for creating special moments between me and this baby that will last far beyond the here and now.

Pregnancy Privilege

*It is God's privilege to conceal things and the king's
privilege to discover them. No one can comprehend
the height of heaven, the depth of the earth,
or all that goes on in the king's mind!*
PROVERBS 25:2–3 NLT

Solomon wrote the book of Proverbs. In it he wrote wise words to help believers live a life devoted to God.

Solomon understood that God knew everything. God saw everything. We humans, who also want to understand everything, have a hard time comprehending the nature of God. But God doesn't need us to know, see, or understand everything. God wants us to trust Him.

As your little baby continues to develop inside of your womb, it's hard to comprehend all that is going on inside of your body. From the hormonal changes, to the development of the placenta, to the continued growth of the baby, it's all going on in the inner workings of your body. A part of you that you can only understand from the looks of the outside of your body.

Reflect on who God is, what He has concealed for you in this pregnancy, and what He is letting you see. Commit to trust Him in this process as your body continues to change.

Father, there are things going on inside of my body that consume me, and there are things going on inside of my body that excite me. I consider this pregnancy a privilege because You are working a miracle right inside of me.

Internal Growth Spurt

That Christ may dwell in your hearts by faith; that ye, being rooted and grounded in love, may be able to comprehend with all saints what is the breadth, and length, and depth, and height; and to know the love of Christ, which passeth knowledge, that ye might be filled with all the fulness of God.
EPHESIANS 3:17–19 KJV

In this scripture, Paul prayed for spiritual growth in the church at Ephesus. He was praying for the power of the Holy Spirit to work in their lives, to lead and guide everything they did.

As an expectant mom, you're also going through a spiritual growth spurt. You're literally experiencing growth as your baby develops. But you're also going through an internal growth spurt. There are certain life lessons that can only be learned through this mommy-to-be calling. You are maturing in the faith.

Consider taking some time in the days and weeks ahead to write down some bold prayers. Journal how God has changed you and your faith perspective. Ask God to help you comprehend what Paul prayed for the Ephesians.

Father, as a result of this pregnancy I want to change from the inside out. Continue to sanctify me to be more like You. Reveal to me great and unsearchable things that I do not know about things to come (Jeremiah 33:2–3). Show me Your ways.

WEEK 12

♡

Believed

Yay! Can you believe it?
You and your baby are nearing
the end of the first trimester!

Overcome My Unbelief

"How long has this been happening?" Jesus asked the boy's father. He replied, "Since he was a little boy. The spirit often throws him into the fire or into water, trying to kill him. Have mercy on us and help us, if you can."
"What do you mean, 'If I can'?" Jesus asked. "Anything is possible if a person believes." The father instantly cried out, "I do believe, but help me overcome my unbelief!"
MARK 9:21–24 NLT

A demon had plagued this boy for quite a while. Jesus helped the father find faith in Him.

In verse 25 (NLT) Jesus spoke. "Listen, you spirit that makes this boy unable to hear and speak," He said. "I command you to come out of this child and never enter him again!"

As a mommy-to-be, you may have areas in your life where you are doubting God. You might be wondering how your family will adjust, or whether the disciplines you are trying to implement with older children will take effect once the new one arrives. In these moments, know that it's okay to talk to God. Thank God for how He already has been faithful to you in the past, and share with Him your needs and concerns for the future (Philippians 4:6–7).

Father, in these moments when I feel consumed by the change that is taking place inside of me, help me to have faith in You to provide everything I need.

Credited Back

*What does Scripture say? "Abraham believed God,
and it was credited to him as righteousness." Now to
the one who works, wages are not credited as a gift
but as an obligation. However, to the one who does
not work but trusts God who justifies the ungodly,
their faith is credited as righteousness.*
ROMANS 4:3–5 NIV

Abraham and his wife, Sarah, tried to take matters into their own hands. They waited and waited on God to give them a son. A promised son who would be their own flesh and blood. But when it was taking way too long, Abraham and Sarah tried to bring about the promise through Sarah's servant, Hagar.

The couple soon realized that they'd created a mess. As they confessed their failures to God and went back to believing what God had originally promised them, He forgave them.

The apostle Paul wrote that because of their faith and trust in God, they were made right with Him once more. God still gave them their promised son!

As a mommy-to-be you will make mistakes too. You're also the daughter of a gracious and merciful God who can forgive anything! You can always bank on that and run back into His arms.

---

*Father, I need You. I need Your help when I've made
the wrong choices. I need Your help to be gracious
with myself when I've messed up and need a time-out.*

From Belief to Resurrection

Against all hope, Abraham in hope believed and so became the father of many nations, just as it had been said to him, "So shall your offspring be." Without weakening in his faith, he faced the fact that his body was as good as dead—since he was about a hundred years old— and that Sarah's womb was also dead.

ROMANS 4:18–19 NIV

Abraham and Sarah got to see their promise come to pass. They had the faith to believe, then experienced weakened faith before their faith was strengthened.

Later on, God asked Abraham to sacrifice this promised son. Out of obedience to God, Abraham brought Isaac before the Lord. Abraham had the faith to believe that if Isaac died, God would somehow raise up—resurrect—Isaac.

In the end, Isaac was saved by God; he didn't have to die. God was testing Abraham to see if he cared more about the promise or the Promise Giver (Genesis 22).

As you walk through this pregnancy, God has great plans in store for you and your baby. But there may be days when you will have to make a conscious choice to believe that there is good in store. Remember that pregnancy is like a resurrection. When you deliver this child, you will get to experience a blessing that far outweighs the discomfort.

Father, help me to believe that You're raising up a blessing inside of me!

SOS

*If you don't know what you're doing, pray to the
Father. He loves to help. You'll get his help, and won't
be condescended to when you ask for it. Ask boldly,
believingly, without a second thought. People who "worry
their prayers" are like wind-whipped waves. Don't think
you're going to get anything from the Master that way,
adrift at sea, keeping all your options open.*
JAMES 1:5–8 MSG

What does it mean to live out your faith under pressure? James wanted believers to know that it was okay to approach God and ask Him for help during any challenging circumstance. James reminded them that God was gracious and merciful—that He would gladly give wisdom and help when needed.

As a mommy-to-be, you also can ask for help when you feel like you're under pressure. When you're tired, weary, perplexed, can't think straight, and wish you had more than two arms and two hands, know that it's okay to ask for help. It's good to ask God for help, and it's good to ask others.

When you feel the tension of whether to ask for help, go to God first. Cry out to Him. He is faithful and knows exactly what you and your baby need.

---

*Lord, thank You that I don't need to make a call
or send You a text in order to receive Your divine
intervention. Thank You for always being right
beside me, ready to help at a moment's notice.*

Believing before Seeing

And Thomas answered and said to Him, "My Lord and my God!" Jesus said to him, "Thomas, because you have seen Me, you have believed. Blessed are those who have not seen and yet have believed."
JOHN 20:28–29 NKJV

Thomas was one of Jesus' twelve disciples. After Jesus was crucified, buried, and resurrected, Thomas doubted. When he learned that Jesus was alive, he couldn't believe it. In fact, he said in verse 25 (NKJV), "Unless I see in His hands the print of the nails, and put my finger into the print of the nails, and put my hand into His side, I will not believe."

Eventually Thomas got to see exactly what he was looking for. He got to see Jesus' body fully resurrected—and then he believed.

At twelve weeks pregnant, you might be wondering if you really are pregnant. You might feel pregnant, but have no baby bump to prove it. Everyone you're telling has said they'll believe it when they see a baby bump.

Or maybe you have all the signs and symptoms that are associated with pregnancy, perhaps even a small bump to prove it.

It might feel like eons from now, but soon enough you will be able to feel your baby moving around inside of you.

Father, thank You for the signs and symptoms that I have (or haven't) had during this pregnancy. I believe You are creating life inside of me. Thank You for using me to create this blessing!

Great Compassion

This was Amanda's second pregnancy. At twelve weeks, she already couldn't believe how different this pregnancy was from her first. She knew many women from the moms' group at church who shared about how different each pregnancy could be.

She didn't feel as nauseous this time around. But she felt more tired and learned her thyroid gland was affected by this pregnancy. So she was put on thyroid medication, and those hormones would be monitored throughout this pregnancy.

Amanda also noticed her baby bump was slowly starting to show. She felt anxious about it, since she didn't notice a baby bump with her first child until well into the second trimester of pregnancy. As a matter of fact, she felt so frustrated about how her body was responding to this pregnancy that she started to cry and began to pray. During her prayers a friend texted her, reminding her that God was with her and that He had great compassion over her situation.

Father, I confess that I don't like how I feel or look right now. I know it's not going to get any easier. But I also know that Your compassion for me is bigger than my expanding body. Please show me just how much You love me today.

A Friend of God

And the scripture was fulfilled which saith,
Abraham believed God, and it was imputed unto him
for righteousness: and he was called the Friend of God.
JAMES 2:23 KJV

Amanda praised God because during her time of prayer, divine intervention took place. As Amanda brought her cares and concerns before God, He prompted her friend to speak truth and life into her spirit.

In the Bible many people were considered friends of God. You too are a friend of God! Do you believe that? Think about it for a moment. What are the characteristics of a best friend? What do you value most in the best friendships you have? What are the qualities and traits of a best friend that you appreciate?

God is like a best friend, but even more! Why? God's love is unconditional, and God speaks truth into your life when you need it the most. Your identity is rooted in what He says about you. Furthermore, if you ever need someone to tell you the honest truth, God will. He's not afraid of what you think, and He has compassion if you don't like what He has to say! And nothing will ever separate you from Him!

So throughout this pregnancy, go to God. He won't let you down!

Father, You're my best friend forever! When I
feel like I'm at my worst during this pregnancy,
I want You to be doing Your best work in my life.

WEEK 13

Encouraged

An encouraging milestone for you
and the baby occurs this week.
It's the end of your first trimester!

Shaped Up

But don't let it faze you. Stick with what you learned and believed, sure of the integrity of your teachers—why, you took in the sacred Scriptures with your mother's milk! There's nothing like the written Word of God for showing you the way to salvation through faith in Christ Jesus. Every part of Scripture is God-breathed and useful one way or another—showing us truth, exposing our rebellion, correcting our mistakes, training us to live God's way. Through the Word we are put together and shaped up for the tasks God has for us.
2 TIMOTHY 3:14–17 MSG

The apostle Paul was in a Roman prison cell when he wrote his second letter to Timothy. He was mentoring Timothy and wrote it to encourage him as he ministered to those in Ephesus.

Mentors help to encourage, lead, and instruct others. As you journey through pregnancy, who do you consider a mentor? Is it the medical staff you're working with? Someone from church? Your mom, grandmother, aunt, cousin, sister, or sister-in-law? A friend, a coworker, or a neighbor? Whoever it may be, consider who God has used in your life to shape you into who you are today. Take some time to thank Him for all of the women, and men, who have helped keep you on the right path.

Father, I want to thank You for all of the people who have helped shape me. As a mommy-to-be, continue to guide me to those who will speak wisdom into my life.

Be Strengthened

*Then the one who looked like a man touched me again,
and I felt my strength returning. "Don't be afraid,"
he said, "for you are very precious to God. Peace! Be
encouraged! Be strong!" As he spoke these words to me,
I suddenly felt stronger and said to him, "Please speak
to me, my lord, for you have strengthened me."*
DANIEL 10:18–19 NLT

The Old Testament prophet Daniel had a dream. It wasn't just any dream. Daniel had been fasting for several days because he wanted to hear from God. He had a dream that spoke directly to him; it was a divine answer to his prayers.

At first Daniel was afraid. But later he was reassured that he didn't need to be scared. Instead, through positive words, he was encouraged. Out of that encouragement came strength and hope to realize his prayers were answered.

So far during this pregnancy, how have you been encouraged? What prayers have you already seen answered? Today, reflect on this gift of encouragement. Think about the past trimester and the good things that have come out of it so far. Who has encouraged you, and how can you be encouraged?

*Father, I need Your divine encouragement. Today I thank
You for helping me make it through this first trimester.
I thank You for the people who have spoken positive
words into my life as a mommy-to-be. Help me to rejoice
and be strengthened as I reflect on Your goodness.*

Consolation Prize

Who comforts (consoles and encourages) us in every trouble (calamity and affliction), so that we may also be able to comfort (console and encourage) those who are in any kind of trouble or distress, with the comfort (consolation and encouragement) with which we ourselves are comforted (consoled and encouraged) by God.
2 CORINTHIANS 1:4 AMPC

A consolation prize can often be misconstrued. It's a prize, usually of minor value, given to the loser or runner-up in a contest, or to all the losers who have performed well or met certain standards.

But as believers in Jesus Christ, we know that a consolation prize is something of great value. It is highly esteemed, not looked down upon. As a mommy-to-be, when you see your children win a consolation prize, you will be excited for them because you know how much it can encourage their little spirits.

While you're pregnant, remember it's okay to give yourself a little consolation prize here and there. It might not look like a ribbon or a medal, but it can be a date night with your spouse, a soak in the bathtub, or a leisurely walk. Remember to do something that will strengthen and encourage your faith, as well as your mental and emotional stamina.

Father, give me wisdom for how to be good to myself during this pregnancy. Show me the best forms of self-care as my body participates in growing this new baby.

An Abundance

Remember this: Whoever sows sparingly will also reap
sparingly, and whoever sows generously will also reap
generously. Each of you should give what you have decided
in your heart to give, not reluctantly or under compulsion,
for God loves a cheerful giver. And God is able to bless you
abundantly, so that in all things at all times, having all that
you need, you will abound in every good work.
2 CORINTHIANS 9:6–8 NIV

Paul encouraged the Corinthians to give generously. Why? Because giving generously meant that God had the opportunity to bless abundantly.

This same principle of sowing generously and reaping generously can be applied to motherhood. When you give your time, talents, and treasure to your baby, you get to experience an abundance of blessings. You might feel tired, but to see the joy on a little baby's face can be the best gift. To hear a baby coo or laugh can be the healing balm to ease the stress of your to-do list.

The more committed and faithful you are to this special mommy-to-be calling, the more God will help you to see the little miracles all around you.

Jesus, open my eyes to see the abundant blessings you
have in store for me. Thank You that this life isn't about
having an abundance of things. Thank You that this life
is about living abundantly by pouring myself out
so that You can fill me back up again.

Not Forgotten

"Can a woman forget her nursing child, and not have compassion on the son of her womb? Surely they may forget, yet I will not forget you. See, I have inscribed you on the palms of My hands; your walls are continually before Me."
ISAIAH 49:15–16 NKJV

You're not a mistake and neither is your baby. You were designed for a purpose. God loves you with an everlasting love (Jeremiah 31:3). You are precious in His sight (Isaiah 43:4).

Take some time to reflect on your childhood. Did you grow up in a safe, nurturing home? No matter how good of a home you were raised in, there were still challenges. As much as your parents loved you, they weren't perfect. But God is!

As a mommy-to-be, you might come into this pregnancy with thoughts and feelings about your childhood: things you want to do differently and things that you believe were done well. No matter what your situation, whether you were loved or rejected, God hasn't forgotten you! Isaiah 49:1, 5 (NLT) says: "The LORD called me before my birth; from within the womb he called me by name. . . . And now the LORD speaks—the one who formed me in my mother's womb to be his servant, who commissioned me to bring Israel back to him. The LORD has honored me, and my God has given me strength."

Father, help me to be the best mommy-to-be that I can be to Your child. Thank You for calling me into this role.

From Distressed to Strengthened

*And David was greatly distressed; for the people spake
of stoning him, because the soul of all the people was
grieved, every man for his sons and for his daughters:
but David encouraged himself in the LORD his God.*

1 SAMUEL 30:6 KJV

David was downcast and rightfully so. He was facing a situation that was hard to fathom in this day and age. But David found strength and encouragement not in himself, but in the Lord. This scripture says it was the Lord his God who provided the encouragement.

Pregnancy comes with its fair share of ups and downs. As you near the end of the first trimester, a part of you might feel downcast about it. Another part of you might be feeling grateful with the hope that better days are ahead of you.

This is a great opportunity to find strength and encouragement from the Lord. God can help you turn any downcast feelings into feelings of fulfillment and courage. When we're encouraged, we're inspired with courage, spirit, or confidence. And we're stimulated by assistance or approval. No matter where you're at today, God approves you. Be encouraged by that!

---

*Lord, You are the great Encourager! Please strengthen
and encourage my faith as I journey through this
pregnancy. Even though I might not feel like I'm at
my best, I trust that You are doing Your best.*

Wonderful Words

*The words of the godly are like sterling silver; the heart of a
fool is worthless. The words of the godly encourage many,
but fools are destroyed by their lack of common sense.*
PROVERBS 10:20–21 NLT

Words can have the ability to strike a chord and penetrate the heart and soul of another person. Solomon wrote in Proverbs 18:21 that the tongue has the power of life and death, and those who love it will eat its fruit.

Your words are powerful! If this isn't your first pregnancy, you probably know just how powerful words can be with your own kids. The way you say something, your tone of voice, and your body language can hold significant value for you and your child. Some doctors indicate that your baby can start to hear sounds inside the womb at eighteen weeks!

As your pregnancy progresses there will be moments (blame it on hormones or the infamous baby brain) when you say something you wish you hadn't. Or you might have meant to say something but you forgot. In those moments, be encouraged by God's grace and mercy to make things right. Even when your words aren't wonderful toward others, if you go to Him, He can help you make things right.

---

*Father, it's by Your grace and mercy that I'm considered
godly, righteous, in Your sight. Thank You for helping me
find the right words to say, even when I can't think straight.*

WEEK 14

♡

Perceived

⌣

Congratulations! You have started
the second trimester. If you have
been dealing with nausea or fatigue,
chances are these symptoms will start
to improve. If this is your second, or
more, pregnancy, you might start
to notice little flutter feelings or
movements from the baby.

Perspective

But thank God! He has made us his captives and continues to lead us along in Christ's triumphal procession. Now he uses us to spread the knowledge of Christ everywhere, like a sweet perfume. Our lives are a Christ-like fragrance rising up to God. But this fragrance is perceived differently by those who are being saved and by those who are perishing.
2 CORINTHIANS 2:14–15 NLT

At fourteen weeks pregnant, Angie was grateful to start feeling better. She couldn't believe what a difference a week or two made for her.

"Lisa, this pregnancy has been so different from my first. The first one I felt like I already gained fifteen pounds by now. With this second pregnancy I haven't gained anything because I've felt so sick."

"I understand, Angie," Lisa said. "I've been there. All three of my pregnancies had different symptoms. I wish there could be a little bit more certainty in all of this. I'm glad to hear you're starting to feel better though."

Angie was so grateful for the moms' group at her church. Conversations like the one with Lisa helped give her perspective, even when she felt unstable, inadequate, or in need of seeing the hands and feet of Jesus in the lives of other moms.

Father, thank You for giving me perspective through other moms and women. Please lead me to the right women who can mentor me as I prepare to have this baby.

Hearing Is Perceiving

For when you did awesome things that we did not
expect, you came down, and the mountains trembled
before you. Since ancient times no one has heard,
no ear has perceived, no eye has seen any God besides
you, who acts on behalf of those who wait for him.

ISAIAH 64:3–4 NIV

"Mommy! Mommy!" shouted Gabby from the top of the staircase.

"What is it?" Mom asked while trying to sit down on the couch in the family room.

"Can the baby hear me at the top of the stairs?"

"Sweetheart, can you please come downstairs so we can talk about your questions?"

"Sure!" Gabby slid down the stairs on her backside.

Once Gabby got into the family room, Mom motioned for her to sit next to her on the couch.

"Why are you so curious about whether or not the baby can hear us?" Mom asked.

"Teacher was talking about our senses today, and I was wondering if the baby can hear us." Gabby patted Mommy's belly.

"Oh, I see." Mom winked her eye. Gabby understood Mom's pun, and she laughed out loud.

"I don't think the baby can start hearing us from inside my belly for a few more weeks."

"Oh, okay. Well, can you let me know when they do? Because I'd like to tell them something."

Father, thank You that I always have access to
talk to You. Thank You for hearing me whether
I speak my prayers out loud or silently.

From Perceived to Received

But Jesus, as He perceived the thoughts of their hearts, took a little child and put him at His side and told them, Whoever receives and accepts and welcomes this child in My name and for My sake receives and accepts and welcomes Me; and whoever so receives Me so also receives Him Who sent Me. For he who is least and lowliest among you all—he is (the one who is truly) great.
LUKE 9:47–48 AMPC

At this stage in your pregnancy, have you had the time to envision what it will be like to hold this child shortly after he or she is born? Chances are you will be overcome with emotions as you receive this beautiful blessing.

Consider how Jesus invites us to recognize and affirm children. When a baby is born they are needy and vulnerable. As you give of yourself to this baby, you will receive so many blessings.

As you continue to prepare for the day you get to accept and welcome this child into the world, ponder the many blessings that await as you also accept and receive the calling to be their mom.

Jesus, in these moments when I feel overwhelmed by the coming arrival of this baby, help prepare me for the blessings You have in store.

Divinely Done

So the wall was finished on the twenty-fifth day of Elul, in fifty-two days. And it happened, when all our enemies heard of it, and all the nations around us saw these things, that they were very disheartened in their own eyes; for they perceived that this work was done by our God.
NEHEMIAH 6:15–16 NKJV

It took fifty-two days, but with some help, Nehemiah led the building of a wall in Jerusalem. When it was complete, the people gave credit to God for His work.

As a mommy-to-be, you have so much to do. Between going to medical appointments, getting ready for the baby, taking on other family and work responsibilities, it all adds up. Sometimes you might wonder how anything will get done once the baby arrives.

Colossians 3:23–24 (NLT) says, "Work willingly at whatever you do, as though you were working for the Lord rather than for people. Remember that the Lord will give you an inheritance as your reward, and that the Master you are serving is Christ."

When you feel the tension is rising like the mercury in a thermometer, you're not alone. Invite God into your role as mommy-to-be. Ask Him for divine wisdom in regard to what needs to get done, how it needs to get done, and who can be involved in the process. You might watch a miracle in the making as things get divinely divided up.

Father, help me as I prepare for this baby. Show me what needs to get done and what can wait.

Noble Character

*She girdeth her loins with strength, and strengtheneth
her arms. She perceiveth that her merchandise is
good: her candle goeth not out by night. She layeth her
hands to the spindle, and her hands hold the distaff.
She stretcheth out her hand to the poor; yea,
she reacheth forth her hands to the needy.*
PROVERBS 31:17–20 KJV

Solomon wrote in Proverbs 31 about the wife of noble character. In it he describes what a godly wife can look like. Solomon
also mentions the husband—one with good character and right
standing with others.

In verses 17–20, Solomon talks about how a godly wife works
and shows compassion toward others. There's a reason why
when a woman goes into labor, it's called labor. It's a lot of
hard, physical work to deliver a baby into this world.

From that point on, having a baby is still a lot of work. With
God's help you can't go wrong. Yes, you'll make mistakes. Yes,
you'll need God's wisdom, but He's right beside you.

As you enter the second trimester, take some time to reflect
on the first trimester. Is there anything in your relationship with
God that you'd like to do differently? Is there anything that's
preventing you from having the kind of character He desires
for you as a mommy-to-be?

*Father, there are twenty-six weeks left to this pregnancy.
As my body continues to develop to deliver this baby,
please develop my character. Sanctify me.
Make me more in Your image.*

You Perceive

You have searched me, LORD, and you know me.
You know when I sit and when I rise; you perceive my
thoughts from afar. You discern my going out and my
lying down; you are familiar with all my ways. Before a
word is on my tongue you, LORD, know it completely.
PSALM 139:1–4 NIV

David wrote Psalm 139. It's a reflection of how God sees you.
How He formed you, made you, shaped you, perceived you.
Psalm 139:13–16 (NIV) says:

> For you created my inmost being;
>   you knit me together in my mother's womb.
> I praise you because I am fearfully and wonderfully made;
>   your works are wonderful,
>   I know that full well.
> My frame was not hidden from you
>   when I was made in the secret place,
>   when I was woven together in the depths of the earth.
> Your eyes saw my unformed body;
>   all the days ordained for me were written in your book
>   before one of them came to be.

Think about it for a moment: Years before you were even conceived, God knew you. He loved you even then. You came
into existence. You grew up with flaws, strengths, pain, and
joy. The same holds true for the baby inside of your belly. Take
some time today to perceive all of these things.

Father, help me to ponder Your ways. It's hard for me to fully
comprehend how You could have loved me before I was
even born. But You did and You still do! Thank You!

Wisdom Is Sweet

My child, eat honey, for it is good, and the honeycomb is sweet to the taste. In the same way, wisdom is sweet to your soul. If you find it, you will have a bright future, and your hopes will not be cut short.
PROVERBS 24:13–14 NLT

"Jake, I don't know how to do this." Abbie shared about her day with her husband after dinner.

"Being pregnant for the third time, with two other little ones at home, is exhausting. By this time with the other two I already felt like I had some energy back."

"I understand. Do you need more help? Should we ask my mom to help, or a neighbor?" Jake asked.

"I don't want to be a burden," Abbie said with tears rolling down her cheeks.

Jake came over and consoled her.

"I get it. I've been having to ask for some help at work lately. It's not easy. I wish I could do it all, or felt like I had the time and energy to do it all. The reality is I just can't. And that's okay."

"I've been praying to God for wisdom about what to do. Sometimes I feel like I just don't know how I'll get through this pregnancy. I'll talk to the neighbors, and you can talk to your parents."

"Sure. That sounds good. Let's pray about this too," Jake added.

Father, please help me to discern how You're leading me through this pregnancy.

WEEK 15

♡

Deemed

As you're settling into your maternity
clothes, your baby can sense light
and is forming taste buds.

Worthy

And the Angel of the Lord appeared to the woman and said to her, Behold, you are barren and have no children, but you shall become pregnant and bear a son.
JUDGES 13:3 AMPC

When it comes to being a mommy-to-be, you might feel like you're walking through some challenges. If it was hard for you to conceive initially, you might be reminded of that season in your life too.

For some women, the first trimester can be challenging. You feel nauseous, exhausted, uncomfortable, and bloated, and you may crave foods you never liked before. You watch your body change shape. To boot, you might also feel hormonal, which means you're more emotional.

As a Christian, you will experience seasons of suffering and sacrifice in order to experience great blessings and rewards. John 16:33 (AMPC) says: "I have told you these things, so that in Me you may have (perfect) peace and confidence. In the world you have tribulation and trials and distress and frustration; but be of good cheer (take courage; be confident, certain, undaunted)! For I have overcome the world. (I have deprived it of power to harm you and have conquered it for you.)"

Your baby is a great reward from the Lord (Psalm 127:3–5)! A precious blessing and a promise that has worth and is worthy of praise.

Father, remind me of this baby's worth and worthiness. Thank You that You consider me worthy enough to carry this baby in my womb.

Deemed Deserving

*This is positive proof of the just and right judgment of God to
the end that you may be deemed deserving of His kingdom
(a plain token of His fair verdict which designs that you
should be made and counted worthy of the kingdom of
God), for the sake of which you are also suffering.*

2 Thessalonians 1:5 AMPC

God has a very high opinion of you, especially as a mommy-
to-be. Did you know that?

He sees you as beautiful, worthy, amazing. In 2 Thessalonians 1:5, the apostle Paul notes that those who follow God
are deemed deserving of His kingdom.

So if a part of you is starting to feel like this pregnancy is
hard and you don't have what it takes, know that with God's
grace you do.

2 Corinthians 4:17–18 (NLT) says, "For our present troubles are
small and won't last very long. Yet they produce for us a glory
that vastly outweighs them and will last forever! So we don't
look at the troubles we can see now; rather, we fix our gaze
on things that cannot be seen. For the things we see now will
soon be gone, but the things we cannot see will last forever."

*Father, You call me Your daughter, Your friend,
and now a mommy-to-be. Thank You for making
me righteous not because of anything I've done
right, but because of what You did on the cross.*

A Wonderful Answer

Behold ye among the heathen, and regard, and wonder marvelously: for I will work a work in your days which ye will not believe, though it be told you.
<small>HABAKKUK 1:5 KJV</small>

Habakkuk was weary and distraught. As a prophet, he felt the weight of concern for the people he served. After Habakkuk expressed his thoughts and opinions to God, God gave him a wonderful and encouraging answer. A hope-filled, reassuring, answer.

It wasn't too long ago that you learned you were pregnant. As your pregnancy has progressed, maybe you have been filled with mixed thoughts and opinions. Like Habakkuk, you can express them. In fact, God wants to hear from you.

Think of a way that you can communicate to God about this pregnancy. Don't be afraid to express what you're thinking. Consider some creative ways you can share these things with God. Here are some ideas:

- Journal or write God a letter.

- Pretend God is sitting next to you and talk to Him.

- Go to a nearby park, sit down on the park bench, and just pray in your heart or out loud.

Whatever you're comfortable with, take some time to express your thoughts. Then wait for God to answer you.

Father, give me the strength to share with You what I've been thinking and feeling during this pregnancy.

The Best Decision

He regarded disgrace for the sake of Christ as of greater value than the treasures of Egypt, because he was looking ahead to his reward. By faith he left Egypt, not fearing the king's anger; he persevered because he saw him who is invisible.
HEBREWS 11:26–27 NIV

Moses had a choice. He could be known as the son of Pharaoh's daughter or he could be mistreated along with God's people. He chose to be among God's people. Through that decision, God blessed Moses immensely. With this decision came great suffering, but also great reward. Moses could have enjoyed the pleasures of this world. But he chose not to.

At this point in your pregnancy, you might already be experiencing the blessings and challenges of your decision to become pregnant. Part of you might be grieving what used to be: a body that wasn't raging with hormones, clothes that fit differently, an appetite that wasn't like a seesaw, or even a good night's sleep. The list might go on and on and cause you to wonder if this was the right decision. By faith, this was the best decision!

In a few short months, this pregnancy will be over. Yes, there will be another season ahead filled with joys and challenges, yet this one will seem like a distant memory.

Jesus, like Moses, help me to have the eyes of faith to see that You are making me a better person as a result of this pregnancy.

Think and Thank

And now, dear brothers and sisters, one final thing.
Fix your thoughts on what is true, and honorable,
and right, and pure, and lovely, and admirable. Think
about things that are excellent and worthy of praise.
Keep putting into practice all you learned and received
from me—everything you heard from me and saw me
doing. Then the God of peace will be with you.
PHILIPPIANS 4:8–9 NLT

Leslie was fifteen weeks into her second pregnancy and really struggling to make sense of it all. This pregnancy had already been a lot harder than her first.

As she shared her frustrations with a newfound friend in a moms' group at church, she began to cry and asked for prayer. The week before, she had to go to the emergency room because she was cramping. Leslie thought something was wrong with the baby. She had to leave her son with a neighbor while she drove herself to the hospital; her husband was on a business trip.

Leslie's friend at the moms' group began to pray for her. Afterward she told Leslie to reach out to her if she needed any help. Leslie was so thankful for the offer, and the two prayed together for God's hand of peace and protection over the remainder of the pregnancy.

Father, help me to remember what the apostle Paul said—
to pray about everything, to tell You what I need,
and to thank You for what You've already done.

Highly Regarded

*And Moses said to Aaron, "This is what the Lord spoke,
saying: 'By those who come near Me I must be
regarded as holy; and before all the people I must
be glorified.'" So Aaron held his peace.*

Leviticus 10:3 nkjv

Candice was already feeling the effects of her fourth pregnancy. Her round ligaments ached and her back hurt. She was exhausted. This pregnancy was a surprise for her and her husband; they thought they were done having kids.

A recent church service message really resonated with her. She felt very broken and didn't know how she was going to make it through another pregnancy.

It was when she received a text from a good friend from her moms' group that her spirits lifted a little bit. It read: Hi Candice! I've been thinking about you. Let's get together soon. I heard you're pregnant again, and I want to find out if there's any way I can help.

Candice instantly felt like fifty pounds had been lifted off of her shoulders. It wasn't everything she had been talking to God about, but she knew it was an answer to meet her needs. Her friend's text motivated her to praise God and to continue to pray for God's help.

---

*Lord, as I continue to walk with You in this pregnancy,
I thank You for meeting all of my needs. Even when
I don't know who will help me, I trust that the
help will ultimately come from You.*

No Matter What

But the LORD was gracious to them, had compassion on them, and regarded them, because of His covenant with Abraham, Isaac, and Jacob, and would not yet destroy them or cast them from His presence.
2 KINGS 13:23 NKJV

Leigh had been having a hard time getting to the moms' group at church. Ever since she became pregnant with her second child, life just overtook her like a tidal wave. Her first trimester was rough: she was sick, exhausted, and could barely remember what day it was.

Now that she was in her second trimester, she prayed things would get better. Leigh was starting to notice little improvements. For one, she was so thankful she could start making it through a church service without needing to run to the restroom. The brain fog seemed to be lifting too.

The rockiness of this pregnancy left her weary though. Her daily devotions felt more like a trivial task than a delightful dose of encouragement. As she read 2 Kings 13:23, she felt a little lift in her spirit. She was reminded that God was gracious and compassionate and regarded her as His daughter no matter what.

Oh Lord, I wish I felt like I was at my best right now. I wish I felt like I was thriving and not just surviving. Father, I trust that You are not only creating a miracle inside of me, but working out a miracle within me.

WEEK 16

♡

Esteemed

As you continue to settle into the second trimester, your baby is settling in as well. Don't be surprised if you notice an increased appetite as your baby will be going through some growth spurts.

Treasured

A good name is more desirable than great riches; to be esteemed is better than silver or gold. Rich and poor have this in common: The LORD is the Maker of them all.
PROVERBS 22:1–2 NIV

Solomon was mindful of his Maker when he wrote this text in Proverbs. He reflected on how God loves humankind. And Solomon found it was wise not to esteem people based on their good works, merits, accomplishments, or wealth. No, a person is highly esteemed because they are made in the image of God, and because God loves them no matter what.

As a Christian, to value human life is a high calling; it is what Christians are called to do. Christians are called to love simply because God loves and accepts them. From Solomon's point of view, this is a much more highly esteemed perspective than to love someone because of their accomplishments or what they can do for you.

As a mommy-to-be, you have a high calling to love a child. From the moment your baby was conceived, to when they come into this world, and every day thereafter, you are called to love. To love no matter what, and to mirror—as best as you can—how God esteems you and them.

Father, this baby of Yours will come into this world completely helpless, with so many needs. Help me to navigate through it all and to love this baby the way You desire me to.

Bless and Expand

There was a man named Jabez who was more honorable than any of his brothers. His mother named him Jabez because his birth had been so painful. He was the one who prayed to the God of Israel, "Oh, that you would bless me and expand my territory! Please be with me in all that I do, and keep me from all trouble and pain!" And God granted him his request.
1 CHRONICLES 4:9–10 NLT

Jabez prayed a prayer asking for God's favor. He prayed for God's blessing, that God would expand his territory. He prayed that God would be with him and keep him from trouble and pain.

Scripture says repeatedly that God is with you. It indicates that God wants to bless you. There are no promises that God will keep you from trouble and pain, but God does have a good purpose for everything (Romans 8:28).

Pregnancy is a time in your life when you will get to experience tremendous blessings. It's also a season in your life when you'll experience great expansion in your heart and body. You can pray that God will keep you from trouble and pain during pregnancy. But you might experience a little of both, and that's okay.

Lord Jesus, thank You for blessing me and expanding my life through the gift of this precious baby inside of me!

His Words

*My foot has held fast to His steps; His ways have I
kept and not turned aside. I have not gone back from
the commandment of His lips; I have esteemed and
treasured the words of His mouth more than my necessary
food. But He is unchangeable, and who can turn Him?
And what He wants to do, that He does.*
JOB 23:11–13 AMPC

Job lost a lot. He went through great anguish and suffering.
But he didn't turn from God. He held on to God as tightly as
he could. Job did everything he could to treasure God's Word
even in the midst of trial. It was as if the Word of God became
Job's food; he couldn't live without it.

No matter what you're going through during this pregnancy,
whether it's been a great one or the most challenging one so far,
God still esteems you. He holds you in high regard and showers
you with His favor.

During pregnancy you might feel a bit out of control. Your
hormones are raging, your body is changing, and it's hard to
think straight. Keep pressing forward, and keep putting one
foot in front of the other. Keep meditating on God's Word,
even when you don't want to. That's when you'll experience
a breakthrough in your relationship with God.

---

*Jesus, help me to remain in Your Word. Fill me up so
that I might overflow to others, including this baby.
May You be highly esteemed and treasured in my life.*

Pregnancy Perspective

God is supremely esteemed. His center holds. Zion brims over with all that is just and right. GOD keeps your days stable and secure—salvation, wisdom, and knowledge in surplus, and best of all, Zion's treasure, Fear-of-GOD.
ISAIAH 33:5–6 MSG

How would your perspective on this pregnancy change if you knew that you were stable and secure? For just a few minutes, don't think about the hormones, pounds already gained, or stretch marks that are starting to appear. Don't think about all of the unknowns like how the last few weeks of this pregnancy will be or how labor and delivery will go. Focus exclusively on who God is for you in your life (Romans 8:31–38).

When you focus on who God is for you in this pregnancy, the ground shifts. That's because He is knitting the baby inside of you. Whether this pregnancy was a surprise or planned, God highly regards you and this baby. That is something to be treasured.

Whether this pregnancy so far has been a breeze or filled with some bizarre twists and turns, He's holding you together. He's at the center of this pregnancy. You are secure. You are stable. You are loved, and so is your baby.

Dear Jesus, please give me Your perspective when it comes to this pregnancy. With so many changes taking place, I want You to be my secure lasting treasure. Help me to live in reverence of You.

God's Glasses

Don't you see that children are GOD's best gift? the fruit of the womb his generous legacy? Like a warrior's fistful of arrows are the children of a vigorous youth. Oh, how blessed are you parents, with your quivers full of children! Your enemies don't stand a chance against you; you'll sweep them right off your doorstep.

PSALM 127:3–5 MSG

From David's perspective, God had His best in mind for you when you got pregnant. It might not always feel like God had His best in mind when you're trying to make it week by week through your pregnancy, or when you endure sleepless nights with your newborn. David tried to see things from God's point of view.

If God wore glasses, what do you think He would see as He looks at you? Now, if He took those glasses off and gave them to you, what do you think you would see? Would you see a miracle in the making? Would you see that the baby inside of you is a generous gift from God? Because a baby is! To have a child is a blessing that reveals that God has great respect and admiration for you, a mommy-to-be.

Father, I want to see this pregnancy from Your perspective. By faith, I receive this child as the best gift You could give me.

Esteeming Him

Jesus said to him, "'You shall love the LORD your God with
all your heart, with all your soul, and with all your mind.'
This is the first and great commandment. And the second
is like it: 'You shall love your neighbor as yourself.' "
MATTHEW 22:37–39 NKJV

Scripture makes it very clear that God loves you. He esteems you! As a mommy-to-be, do you receive that? If you receive it, are you able to extend that grace to others? To your other children, spouse, neighbors, friends, and acquaintances?

These are some hard questions to wrestle with. Depending on your background and your current circumstances, there might be a place in your heart that isn't sure how to receive the goodness of God. You might also be hesitant to extend that goodness to others.

As you read this devotional, consider that you're trying to regard God and make Him a priority in your life. Take some time today to pray or journal and consider these questions for reflection:

- How can I make God a priority in my life before this baby comes into the world?

- How can I continue to make God a priority in my life after this baby is born?

Father, to be the best mommy I can be for this baby,
I first need to make You a priority. If I haven't,
please forgive me. Now help me to move forward
loving You with all of my heart, soul, and mind.

In or Out

And these words, which I command thee this day, shall be in thine heart: and thou shalt teach them diligently unto thy children, and shalt talk of them when thou sittest in thine house, and when thou walkest by the way, and when thou liest down, and when thou risest up. And thou shalt bind them for a sign upon thine hand, and they shall be as frontlets between thine eyes. And thou shalt write them upon the posts of thy house, and on thy gates.
DEUTERONOMY 6:6–9 KJV

"My family were CEO Christians," Agnes shared with her new mentor mom. "You know: Christmas and Easter only. Now I hold God in high regard. Ben and I go to church every week. We're a part of a community group, and we volunteer at the church. I'm in God's Word maybe two to three times a week at best."

"So why are you sharing this with me, Agnes?"

"This is my first baby, and what if we won't be able to live out our faith?"

"Agnes, things will change when this newborn arrives. But I believe that if you and Ben esteem God, then He will help you. Let's ask God for wisdom for how to stay in His Word on a regular basis. If you can start this discipline, I believe you'll be able to continue it after the baby is born."

Father, as a mommy-to-be, I want to be in. I want to stay committed to You!

WEEK 17

Admired

If you have had a hard time
deciphering whether you can feel
your baby move or kick, chances
are you'll start to notice and admire
those movements now.

In Awe

Esther was the daughter of Abihail, who was Mordecai's uncle. (Mordecai had adopted his younger cousin Esther.) When it was Esther's turn to go to the king, she accepted the advice of Hegai, the eunuch in charge of the harem. She asked for nothing except what he suggested, and she was admired by everyone who saw her.

ESTHER 2:15 NLT

Jackie didn't gain a lot of weight during her two pregnancies, so she was able to bounce back into her pre-pregnancy clothes shortly thereafter.

Several women in the moms' group Jackie attended at church didn't know how she was able to do it: have two little ones and be active postpartum. Until the day Jackie had the chance to share her testimony at the moms' group.

The women stopped being jealous or envious of Jackie and learned to admire her. They learned that prior to her first pregnancy, she was diagnosed with an autoimmune condition that made it challenging to conceive and give birth to a healthy, full-term child. They also learned that Jackie was an athlete growing up, so she had the discipline of living an active lifestyle. Through Jackie, they learned not to compare themselves as moms but to have compassion for each mom's circumstances, regardless of their outward appearance.

Father, when I'm tempted to compare myself to other pregnant or postpartum moms, help me to admire You first and foremost. Help me to be in awe of the work You're doing in their lives.

Who's in Charge?

*GOD is in charge of human life, watching and examining us
inside and out. Love and truth form a good leader; sound
leadership is founded on loving integrity. Youth may be
admired for vigor, but gray hair gives prestige to old age.*
PROVERBS 20:27–29 MSG

"I didn't even know if I would be able to have kids," Jackie
shared with the moms' group. "And to be honest, before I
learned about my health condition, I struggled with the idea
of having children."

"I did too," one of the other women in the group said.

"Me too," another one added.

Jackie was surprised but also comforted by the reality that
she had the same thoughts and feelings about motherhood.
When she was a child she dreamed of becoming a mom. She
would play dress-up and pretend that she was a mom to several kids. She watched reruns of *The Brady Bunch* and thought
about how exciting it must have been to have so many children
in one house.

But as Jackie grew up and got married, life and responsibilities settled in. The reality of having a lot of children felt
daunting. Who would really be in charge of it all? God would
be, and that gave Jackie some peace of mind.

---

*Jesus, I admire Your ways and how You create life. I desire
to be a mommy-to-be of integrity—a mommy-to-be whom
others will admire for yielding the gift of life into Your hands.*

From Broken to Wooed

When He comes to be glorified in His saints (on that day He will be made more glorious in His consecrated people), and (He will) be marveled at and admired (in His glory reflected) in all who have believed (who have adhered to, trusted in, and relied on Him), because our witnessing among you was confidently accepted and believed (and confirmed in your lives).
2 Thessalonians 1:10 AMPC

"When I learned that this condition could make it challenging to conceive or give birth to a healthy child, I wanted children," Jackie shared with the moms' group.

"It wasn't until I felt like being a mom could be taken away from me that I wanted to be one," Jackie added.

"Just like how I had to become broken in order to receive Christ into my life, I also had to continually be broken and wooed by Him to receive the blessings He had for me."

The moms took some time to think about how they accepted Jesus Christ into their lives. Some of the moms recalled how broken they were when they accepted Christ. They continued to be wooed by God because they admired His attributes; they wanted to implement those characteristics into their own lives as moms.

Father, as a mommy-to-be I still feel broken. Help me to remember the day I turned my heart over to You. Continue to woo me so that I can be the best mom for this baby.

Mommy Mentor

Saul and Jonathan—in life they were loved and admired, and in death they were not parted. They were swifter than eagles, they were stronger than lions.
2 Samuel 1:23 niv

As Jackie wrapped up her message for the moms' group, one of the leaders stood up to pray for the group. She then prompted the group of moms to consider who had been a mentor in their lives. Afterward, she asked some of the older moms in the room to spread out among the tables and sit next to a mom they didn't know.

During that time, the older moms mingled with the younger moms. Some of the newer moms in the room were pregnant, while many of the other moms were just a few months postpartum. As the older moms conversed with the younger ones, Jackie noticed something beautiful. She could see that all of the women admired each other.

As the moms' meeting came to a close, one of the leaders let Jackie pray. As she prayed, her heart felt open and receptive to what God had in store for this group of women.

Jesus, please help lead me to a group of moms that I can relate to and share my faith with. Lead me to moms who can be mentors and moms who can be friends. I know You are with me and I can't live out this calling alone.

Secret Admirer

Observe people who are good at their work—
skilled workers are always in demand and admired;
they don't take a backseat to anyone.
PROVERBS 22:29 MSG

As the moms' group meeting ended, Jackie walked up to one of the older moms, Leah. She had noticed that Leah had a way about her that was admirable. Leah was about seventeen weeks pregnant with her fourth child, and she was devoted to her husband and family. Leah served the church and the moms' group in a number of different ways.

"Leah, I've been watching you. How you interact with your husband and children. I was wondering, would you ever be interested in getting together for some coffee?" Jackie asked.

"Sure, I'd love to," Leah agreed.

"Great. By the way—congrats on the baby! How have you been feeling?"

"I'm doing okay, Jackie. Thanks for asking. I feel like there are things about each pregnancy that just get more challenging. I think it's because I have other little ones to manage."

"Sure. Well, just know that I greatly admire you. When we meet I'd love to talk about how you felt led to have more babies. I'm not sure if Dan and I are done yet. I feel like I need some wisdom from someone like you."

"I'd love to share more with you," Leah said.

Father, I'm grateful I followed the calling to become
a mommy-to-be. Thank You for the women and moms
who have been admirable examples to me.

Approved

There's no one like her on earth, never has been, never will be. She's a woman beyond compare. My dove is perfection, pure and innocent as the day she was born, and cradled in joy by her mother. Everyone who came by to see her exclaimed and admired her—all the fathers and mothers, the neighbors and friends, blessed and praised her.
SONG OF SOLOMON 6:8–9 MSG

Mandy was seventeen weeks pregnant. Those who knew she was expecting her second child thought she looked fantastic. She was radiating with that pregnancy glow that some moms rave about. On the outside Mandy might have looked great, but in reality, she didn't feel good. A couple of weeks before, she'd ended up in the emergency room. While she wasn't cramping, she did start to bleed. None of her doctors really knew what caused the disruption. So now Mandy was praying through a lot of fears and unknowns. Then her husband prayed for her.

"God, Mandy and I need you. We believe this child is Yours. We are asking for Your strength and help to see it come full-term. Grant us Your favor and peace during this time."

From that moment on, Mandy committed to pray for this baby. She knew her baby was approved by God for a purpose, and she was excited to be a mom again.

Father, during pregnancy there are things some people can't explain. Thank You for calling me Your daughter and for approving me.

A Woman Who Fears the Lord

Her children rise up and call her blessed; her husband also,
and he praises her: "Many daughters have done well,
but you excel them all." Charm is deceitful and beauty
is passing, but a woman who fears the Lord, she shall
be praised. Give her of the fruit of her hands,
and let her own works praise her in the gates.
PROVERBS 31:28–31 NKJV

The writer of Proverbs 31 felt that it was important to write about what to look for in a noble wife. This text extols many characteristics and attributes regarding being a woman, wife, and mom. But one of the most important attributes is fear of the Lord.

As a mommy-to-be, portraying a reverence for God shows that you know who's in control of your life as well as your baby's life. While you might be carrying this baby in your womb, it's God who is truly carrying and creating this child.

At times you might find yourself in awe of who God is and yet wanting to be (or perhaps believing that you are) in control. Take some time today to reflect on the many attributes of God and submit to His authority.

Father, I want to surrender myself to You.
During this unique experience, I want to view being a
mommy-to-be as an opportunity to be part of a miracle.

WEEK 18

♡

Treasured

In the next few weeks you might be able to get a peek at your baby's gender and walk away with a treasured ultrasound picture. Also, if you haven't had to start wearing maternity clothes yet, from here on out you might due to an increased appetite and baby's growth spurts.

A Precious Jewel

"On the day when I act," says the LORD Almighty, "they will be my treasured possession. I will spare them, just as a father has compassion and spares his son who serves him. And you will again see the distinction between the righteous and the wicked, between those who serve God and those who do not."
MALACHI 3:17–18 NIV

Malachi was a prophet who spoke about serving God with reverence and awe. What does serving God with reverence look like?

If you have put your faith and hope in a life-giving and life-saving relationship with Jesus Christ, chances are you are already serving in some capacity. As a mommy-to-be you are developing another area of service by loving and caring for this child God has given you. Although having a baby will change your perspective, to serve this child will open the doors for you to bear much fruit for God's kingdom.

If you love to serve but know that once the baby comes you will have to adjust some of your commitments, don't be hard on yourself if you have to reassess. Remember that God has great compassion for you during this season of life. He considers you a precious jewel—a treasure.

Father, as I prepare for the arrival of this baby, please give me wisdom for knowing what to say yes to and what to say no to. Help me to be gracious with myself as I make these decisions.

Loved Lavishly

How blessed is God! And what a blessing he is! He's the Father of our Master, Jesus Christ, and takes us to the high places of blessing in him. Long before he laid down earth's foundations, he had us in mind, had settled on us as the focus of his love, to be made whole and holy by his love. Long, long ago he decided to adopt us into his family through Jesus Christ. (What pleasure he took in planning this!) He wanted us to enter into the celebration of his lavish gift-giving by the hand of his beloved Son.
EPHESIANS 1:3–6 MSG

If you treasure something, you treat it as precious and cherish it. The apostle Paul wrote to the church in Ephesus about how much God loved them. God chose them, adopted them, and called them His own. All of this before He even laid down the foundations of the earth! He considered us chosen, set apart as holy and righteous.

Long before you were born, God loved you with an everlasting love. Long before the baby in your womb was conceived, he or she was loved!

To know that you and your baby are loved is something to celebrate. No matter what's going on in your life, take some time to celebrate the fact that God loves you.

Father, sometimes I feel like I've just scratched the surface in understanding how much You love me and this little baby. Lord, show me just how much You love me today.

A Dedication

*But her gain and her hire (the profits of Tyre's new prosperity)
will be dedicated to the Lord (eventually); it will not be
treasured or stored up, for her gain will be used for those
who dwell in the presence of the Lord (the ministers), that
they may eat sufficiently and have durable and stately
clothing (suitable for those who minister at God's altar).*
ISAIAH 23:18 AMPC

Within the next few days or weeks you might decide whether or not to find out the gender of your baby. Whatever you decide, one question to start thinking about is this: How do you want to dedicate your child to the Lord?

Depending on your church denomination, after your baby is born you might get your child baptized or dedicated or decide to wait until your child is old enough to make the decision for themselves.

While you will certainly treasure your child, consider them precious, and cherish them, start praying about how you can celebrate this life before the One who gave it. To dedicate your baby is a way to publicly declare that you'll embrace teaching your child about Jesus. It's also a significant milestone as a parent to dedicate this child to the Lord.

---

*Father, although I haven't seen this child face-to-face
yet, I treasure them. But help me not to forget
whose they really are. In the days and weeks ahead,
please show me how to dedicate my baby back to You.*

Treasure Chest

So they hurried off and found Mary and Joseph, and the baby, who was lying in the manger. When they had seen him, they spread the word concerning what had been told them about this child, and all who heard it were amazed at what the shepherds said to them. But Mary treasured up all these things and pondered them in her heart.
Luke 2:16–19 NIV

Growing up, did you have a treasure chest in your room? Perhaps a place, a box, or a drawer where you kept what were considered your most prized possessions? If you had a special place to put these items, do you remember what you included? Perhaps an award, a ribbon, a medal, a piece of jewelry, a picture, a rock?

Having a special place to put these things meant that you cherished them and treated them with favor, respect, honor, perhaps even wonder.

In Luke chapter 2 we read that Mary created a treasure chest right inside of her chest; more specifically in her heart. She didn't have a specific place where she could put her memories, so she thought about them and kept them close to her, right on the inside of her.

Take some time to think about your baby today. Talk to them. Tell them about your hopes and dreams for them. Say a prayer out loud over them.

Father, show me how I can treasure this baby not just with things but with spiritual awe and wonder.

Precious Possession

For you know that God paid a ransom to save you from
the empty life you inherited from your ancestors. And it
was not paid with mere gold or silver, which lose their
value. It was the precious blood of Christ, the sinless,
spotless Lamb of God. God chose him as your ransom
long before the world began, but now in these last
days he has been revealed for your sake.
1 PETER 1:18–20 NLT

God loves you, but did you know that He bought you? He
paid a ransom for you and your baby. What was this ransom?
It wasn't something that was paid for with silver, gold, or other
valuable possessions. No. This ransom was God allowing His one
and only Son, Jesus, to die on the cross for the forgiveness of
your sins. It was the sacrifice of the perfect Lamb. Jesus' blood
paid the ransom.

There's nothing you can do to pay God back for this ransom.
There's no good works you can do to justify what happened at
Calvary. All God wants for you, as a mommy-to-be, is to accept
that His precious possession can now be yours.

Most days as a mommy-to-be this revelation isn't an easy
one to accept or even remember. But God's grace and mercy
invite you to live it out.

Father, help me to adore the most precious possession
I'll ever have on this side of heaven: a relationship
with Your Son, Jesus. Thank You for Your love.

Hide and Seek

*Again, the kingdom of heaven is like unto treasure
hid in a field; the which when a man hath found,
he hideth, and for joy thereof goeth and selleth
all that he hath, and buyeth that field.*
MATTHEW 13:44 KJV

At eighteen weeks pregnant, Meredith couldn't wait to find out the gender of her baby. Hers was considered a high-risk pregnancy, so to ensure the well-being of her and the baby, things had to be closely monitored.

This pregnancy wasn't an easy road for her and her husband, Seth. They already had two children, but felt like they were supposed to have more. While trying to conceive, they miscarried two times—and knew heartache they'd never experienced before.

But this pregnancy seemed to be going well despite the previous circumstances. Meredith already had a girl and a boy, but she was still curious to know the gender. At her most recent appointment she walked away with several ultrasound images. She looked at them to see if she could find the gender. Unfortunately, the baby was playing hide-and-seek in many of the images, so it was hard to tell. Overall, though, Meredith was filled with great joy for this baby, and she praised God.

---

*Father, thank You for miracle babies. They remind
me that nothing is impossible with You, and they
remind me how fragile this life inside of me is.*

Stockpile

Before becoming pregnant with her third child, Meredith held on to a lot of baby stuff. There were piles upon piles, boxes upon boxes of baby things set aside in their basement. Because she and Seth believed they were meant to have a third child, they held on to everything.

When Meredith and Seth miscarried, they decided to slowly get rid of their stockpile of baby treasures. Friends and family who were expecting were blessed with the baby items. Giving everything they had away helped Meredith and Seth to feel blessed with the children they already had and to let go of having more children.

When they learned they were finally pregnant with their third, it felt like such a surprise. They praised God for this gift, because they knew their treasure wasn't just the gift of life, but the One who graced them with this gift.

Lord, help me to remember that the baby inside of me isn't from my own good works or something I created. This baby is life that You created and is truly a gift from You! Thank You!

WEEK 19

♡

Loved

You're almost halfway through your pregnancy! If you like to sing out loud, go ahead and sing a love song to your baby. Chances are they might be able to hear you!

Reverence

As a father has compassion on his children, so the Lord has compassion on those who fear him; for he knows how we are formed, he remembers that we are dust.
PSALM 103:13–14 NIV

As a mommy-to-be, you might have a lot of fears—fears of the unknown. Sometimes your fears are valid, but often they never become a reality.

One fear you may be struggling with is fear of man. But God tells us, especially through David in the Psalms, that it isn't man we should fear; it's God. When we fear God though, it needs to look a lot different than the way we might fear people or things in this world. A reverence for God is a more accurate description of how we should view God and love Him. Reverence is an attitude of deep respect tinged with awe.

In Psalm 103, David writes about how God is a father to you. Like a father who has compassion for his children, God also has compassion for those who love and display reverence for Him. God formed you, and He knows how you were formed.

To know that the power of life comes from God alone is amazing! Give Him praise.

Father, You are worthy of my praise. Help me to live in reverence of You. Help me to teach my baby also to live with a deep love, respect, and admiration for You.

Copycat

But from everlasting to everlasting the LORD's love is
with those who fear him, and his righteousness with
their children's children—with those who keep his
covenant and remember to obey his precepts.
PSALM 103:17–18 NIV

Leigh needed some time to read the Bible. As her daughter was playing in the family room, Leigh sat down on the couch and started to read.

"Mommy, can I read with you?" her inquisitive five-year-old asked her.

"Sure thing, sweetheart."

At nineteen weeks pregnant, Leigh already had a little baby bump. Her daughter had to sit to the side of her instead of on her lap.

"Mommy, I'm going to get my Bible too. This way we can read our Bibles together. I love God because you do too."

"That sounds like a great idea!" Leigh said.

Leigh smiled from ear to ear. In her heart she thanked God for her daughter and this new baby inside of her womb. She prayed that God would help her to be a witness to her children; to reflect God's love, grace, and mercy so that it might lead them to have a reverence for God.

Father, being a mommy-to-be isn't just about having a baby.
It's an opportunity to expand my heart to love You more and
to minister to and witness to life. Help me to love this baby
and be a witness to them. Most importantly, I pray that Your
grace and mercy will fill in the gaps where I fall short.

Faith Fruit

But the fruit of the Spirit is love, joy, peace, longsuffering, kindness, goodness, faithfulness, gentleness, self-control. Against such there is no law.
GALATIANS 5:22–23 NKJV

At this stage in your pregnancy, you may have already read countless articles, books, and apps explaining the many benefits of eating well during your pregnancy. All of this information is good for you and your body. Fruit, especially, will provide you and your baby with a lot of nourishment in the days and weeks ahead.

The same is true in your spiritual walk as a mommy-to-be. Figurative faith fruit is an essential part of your relationship with God. The *Message* translation puts Galatians 5:22–23 this way:

> But what happens when we live God's way? He brings gifts into our lives, much the same way that fruit appears in an orchard—things like affection for others, exuberance about life, serenity. We develop a willingness to stick with things, a sense of compassion in the heart, and a conviction that a basic holiness permeates things and people. We find ourselves involved in loyal commitments, not needing to force our way in life, able to marshal and direct our energies wisely.

As a mommy-to-be, make a commitment to pray boldly to love so that faith fruit may overflow from the inside out.

Father, I want to love this baby the way You desire me to and the way this baby needs me to. Help me to bear much fruit for You.

Counterintuitive Love

When Israel was a child, then I loved him and called My son out of Egypt. The more (the prophets) called to them, the more they went from them; they kept sacrificing to the Baals and burning incense to the graven images. Yet I taught Ephraim to walk, taking them by their arms or taking them up in My arms, but they did not know that I healed them.
HOSEA 11:1–3 AMPC

God called the prophet Hosea to do something counterintuitive. Something completely and totally out of this world. Was the task impossible? From a worldly perspective, yes. From God's perspective, no.

What was it that God asked of Hosea? To love with a counterintuitive, supernatural love. God called Hosea to marry Gomer. But Gomer wasn't just any woman; she was a prostitute. Even though Gomer remained unfaithful to Hosea for quite a while, God continued to call Hosea to love Gomer. To woo her back. To forgive her.

As a mommy-to-be, you have your flaws too. Perhaps you have struggled at times in your relationship with your spouse. Maybe you have even struggled in your relationship with God. There's so much hope in the story between Hosea and Gomer. God loves you enough to forgive you and welcome you back.

Father, as a mommy-to-be I can be so wayward. I'm sorry for falling short, for doing what I know I shouldn't do. Please forgive me. Thank You for accepting me.

Sacrificial Love

*God showed how much he loved us by sending his one
and only Son into the world so that we might have eternal
life through him. This is real love—not that we loved God,
but that he loved us and sent his Son as a sacrifice to take
away our sins. Dear friends, since God loved us that much,
we surely ought to love each other.*

1 John 4:9–11 NLT

God sacrificed His one and only Son so that you can enter
into a relationship with Him and have eternal life. Think for a
moment what that must have been like for God to sacrifice
His beloved Son.

If anyone knows what it's like to endure longsuffering for
their child, it's God. Other moms will attest to the fact that being
a mommy-to-be is a time filled with some of life's greatest joys
and challenges. God knows this too.

Take some time today to think about this sacrifice that God
endured for you and your baby. Praise Him that because He
laid down His life, you get to enjoy God forever! Pray that your
baby will someday make the same decision to accept Christ.

---

*Father, thank You that because of what Your Son did on the
cross at Calvary, You understand sacrificial love better than
anybody I know. As a mommy-to-be I know exactly who to go
to when I feel the weight of parenting on my shoulders: You!*

A Catalyst

God so loved the world, that he gave his only begotten Son, that whosoever believeth in him should not perish, but have everlasting life. For God sent not his Son into the world to condemn the world; but that the world through him might be saved.

JOHN 3:16–17 KJV

John wanted to make something very clear to his audience: God loves everyone. Because God loves everyone, He wanted to save everyone.

In your life, what has been a catalyst for love? What has driven you to a place where you want to express love toward others? Another form of expressing the love you have is by being a mommy-to-be.

Maybe your motivation for becoming a mommy-to-be is that you always knew you wanted to have children. Maybe you wanted to raise your children differently and give them opportunities you didn't have growing up. These motivations have an underlying theme, a catalyst—love.

Jesus was motivated by the same thing. He knew what He was called to do. He asked His Father to pass the cup of crucifixion from Him, but accepted His Father's will and endured it for the sake of love.

Father, I'm almost halfway through this pregnancy. There are things about this pregnancy I wish You would take away. But I'm doing this for love, so help me to endure, knowing there is a blessing at the end.

Resurrection Coming

*My old self has been crucified with Christ. It is no longer I
who live, but Christ lives in me. So I live in this earthly body
by trusting in the Son of God, who loved me and gave
himself for me. I do not treat the grace of God as
meaningless. For if keeping the law could make us right
with God, then there was no need for Christ to die.*
GALATIANS 2:20–21 NLT

The apostle Paul wrote to the Christian communities in Galatia.
He taught how his past had died with Christ. That Christ lived
in him, and because of that he had hope. Hope of a new life
now and in eternity.

Pregnancy can be considered longsuffering, patient endurance. There's a part of you that slowly dies to self. As you lay
yourself down for the sake of another, that being your baby,
you get to experience change, grief, loss. But on the other
side of delivery, and in the life to come of this child, you get
to experience blessings, new life, a resurrection.

By God's grace, there's a resurrection coming for you!

---

*Father, this pregnancy has already had its ups and downs.
At times I've enjoyed it, and at times I wish it were over.
Please grant me the patience I need to endure. I'm looking
forward to the new life that will be on the other side.*

WEEK 20

Refreshed

Congratulations! You're halfway through your pregnancy, which might feel mentally refreshing.

Halfway Mark

The LORD is my shepherd, I lack nothing. He makes me lie down in green pastures, he leads me beside quiet waters, he refreshes my soul. He guides me along the right paths for his name's sake.
PSALM 23:1–3 NIV

Like running a marathon or participating in any endurance-related sport, it's always refreshing to know you're at the halfway mark. The finish line is in sight! God's grace has carried you and your baby this far and will continue to do so.

As you reach twenty weeks gestation, now is a great time to take a mommy-to-be inventory. How are you feeling? Are you starting to plan ahead to the due date? Here are some things to be thinking about, and praying over, in the next week or two:

- What am I doing daily that is good for me physically, emotionally, and spiritually?

- What am I doing daily that is good for the baby physically, emotionally, and spiritually?

- Am I taking some time to pray for this baby?

- Have I started to get the nursery ready?

- What plans do I have in place for when the baby arrives?

- Who do I feel comfortable asking to help me after the baby arrives?

- Have I started to pray about a first and middle name for this baby?

Father, by Your grace and mercy alone, I thank You I've made it to the halfway mark in this pregnancy!

Please and Thank You

And I am praying that you will put into action the generosity that comes from your faith as you understand and experience all the good things we have in Christ. Your love has given me much joy and comfort, my brother, for your kindness has often refreshed the hearts of God's people.
PHILEMON 1:6–7 NLT

April was so grateful to finally be twenty weeks pregnant. She couldn't wait to find out the gender of her third child. So far, this pregnancy had had many ups and downs. During the first few weeks of pregnancy, she thought she was going to lose the baby. But thanks to the care and compassion of a highly trained medical team, she was doing much better.

As a result of the complications during her first trimester, and being at high risk due to her age, she had to do some modified bed rest. Although April felt weary and anxious, she did her best to show kindness to—and even share her faith with—some of the medical team.

Reaching the halfway point in her third pregnancy felt like crossing a huge hurdle. April knew there was still a long way to go, but in this moment she was very thankful for all that God had provided for her and the baby.

Father, during this pregnancy I pray that gentleness and kindness will shine through my spirit and refresh the hearts of others.

Renewed

I want you to know how delighted I am to have
Stephanas, Fortunatus, and Achaicus here with me.
They partially make up for your absence! They've
refreshed me by keeping me in touch with you.
Be proud that you have people like this among you.
1 CORINTHIANS 16:17–18 MSG

April received a text message from a good friend from the moms' group she was a part of at church. It read: HI APRIL! CONGRATS ON MAKING IT TO 20 WEEKS! I WAS WONDERING IF YOU'D LIKE FOR ME TO WATCH THE KIDS WHEN YOU GO IN FOR YOUR GENDER REVEAL ULTRASOUND THIS WEEK? LET ME KNOW. I'D BE HAPPY TO HELP YOU OUT!

This text message from Jasmine was a huge answer to April's prayers. With her husband out of town on a business trip and her in-laws away for a family wedding, she wondered who would watch her kids.

In this moment, April was so grateful for the moms' group. Sometimes it was a lot of work to get out of the house, just to get to the group. But she always felt like it was exactly what she needed every time she went.

Father, thank You for the moms in my life. Moms I can do life
with, laugh with, and cry with. Women who are in the same
season of life as me, which helps me not to feel alone.

RSVP

*The (Holy) Spirit and the bride (the church, the true
Christians) say, Come! And let him who is listening say,
Come! And let everyone come who is thirsty (who is painfully
conscious of his need of those things by which the soul is
refreshed, supported, and strengthened); and whoever
(earnestly) desires to do it, let him come, take, appropriate,
and drink the water of Life without cost.*
REVELATION 22:17 AMPC

John had a revelation. Coming to faith was a free gift. With the acceptance of this free gift came an abundance of refreshment. Being refreshed provides you with new vigor and energy.

When you received this invitation into your life, how did you RSVP? Did you say yes or no? Did you say yes, but wavered in the faith? Did you say no, but regretted that decision?

Here's an opportunity for you to receive the invitation again. As a mommy-to-be, you need some time to be refreshed. Being refreshed is going to look a whole lot different now than it did over twenty weeks ago. But God can still meet you wherever you're at. Jesus offers refreshment. Go to Him. Cling to Him. Find Him again.

---

*Dear Jesus, I want to rest in You. During pregnancy,
I'm not so sure how to do that. It's hard to rest.
Please provide moments for me to become refreshed.
I'm choosing to RSVP to You today.*

Go with the Flow

He that believeth on me, as the scripture hath said,
out of his belly shall flow rivers of living water. (But this
spake he of the Spirit, which they that believe on him
should receive: for the Holy Ghost was not yet given;
because that Jesus was not yet glorified.)
JOHN 7:38–39 KJV

Amber was grateful to be getting ready to attend the moms' group meeting. She was looking forward to hearing the speaker talk about John 7:38–39.

Prior to leaving her house, she had a lot to get done. Between preschool drop-off and stopping at the grocery store to pick up some food to contribute to the meeting, she felt a bit weary.

"This used to be so much easier when I wasn't pregnant. Now I have to plan for going to the bathroom sometime in between dropping Hannah off and picking up the food," she told Meredith, her co-leader, over the phone.

"I totally get it, Amber. Just come as you are. We won't start without you. If you're a few minutes late, that's okay. We'll see you soon."

"And I'm getting out of breath a lot faster these days. Can you meet me at the front entrance when I get here?"

"Sure, just text me when you arrive."

Father, while I'm thankful to be halfway through
this pregnancy, new symptoms are starting to
emerge that I wish would go away. Please help
me to go with the flow and trust You with my body.

Good Company

So that by God's will I may subsequently come to you with joy (with a happy heart) and be refreshed (by the interval of rest) in your company. May (our) peace-giving God be with you all! Amen (so be it).
ROMANS 15:32–33 AMPC

Amber made it to moms' group just in time. As she made her way through the hallways and back to the community room where the moms' group was going to meet, she ran into the guest speaker.

"I was wondering if I could sit with you guys during brunch? And then before I speak, can we pray?"

"Absolutely. I have a devotion I was going to read before you speak, so I'll make sure to pray afterward too. I'll be sitting with Meredith at the table closest to the podium."

As the moms made their way into the community room and started eating breakfast, Amber got to know more about the guest speaker. How she just learned that she was a few weeks pregnant with her second, and how she was struggling with terrible morning sickness.

"Well, you're in good company, because I'm twenty weeks pregnant today. I'm just starting to feel better!" Amber shared with the speaker.

Father, I know Your Word says over and over again that I'm not alone, but sometimes I forget. Thank You for Your reminders that gently nudge me to know I'm in good company.

Good for the Soul

A generous person will prosper;
whoever refreshes others will be refreshed.
PROVERBS 11:25 NIV

"Ladies, please join me in a word of prayer," Amber said.

The moms' group took some time to pray over Joy, the speaker. They prayed for strength, favor, and the ability to speak well.

Joy did an awesome job ministering to the moms. She focused the message on her testimony, teaching from John 7:38–39. Joy emphasized the importance of being refreshed by God's Word and that the only way that can happen is if a person remains in God's Word daily.

At the close of Joy's message, she prayed for the moms. Then Amber got up to pray for Joy again. As she did, Amber was led to pray Proverbs 11:25 over Joy. Within the text is a promise that whoever is generous in refreshing others will be refreshed. Amber believed that through Joy's act of obedience—speaking into the lives of the moms—God would bless and minister to Joy in a powerful way. That what Joy did, speaking when she barely had the strength, was actually really good for her soul.

Jesus, thank You for using me in my weaknesses.
As a mommy-to-be, sometimes I feel so inadequate.
But help me to remember that if I step out in faith to
bless others, You will also prosper and refresh me.

WEEK 21

Strengthened

If you haven't started to feel your baby move by now, chances are you will soon. In the weeks to come the movements will become stronger and more forceful.

Fortified

A woman, when she gives birth to a child, has grief (anguish, agony) because her time has come. But when she has delivered the child, she no longer remembers her pain (trouble, anguish) because she is so glad that a man (a child, a human being) has been born into the world. So for the present you are also in sorrow (in distress and depressed); but I will see you again and (then) your hearts will rejoice, and no one can take from you your joy (gladness, delight).
JOHN 16:21–22 AMPC

Diana's OB confirmed that she had low iron in her blood. To improve her iron deficiency, Diana would need to adjust her diet and take a daily iron supplement.

Diana was already taking a daily prenatal vitamin with iron. Now she was going to have to take even more iron to keep her body, and her baby's body, strong.

Diana's OB helped her see the positive in this situation: Diana would only need to make these changes during her pregnancy. Her OB also said they would check her iron count at the next prenatal appointment. If things improved, Diana might not need to take the daily supplement anymore.

Lord, during this pregnancy, You are my strength. No matter what unexpected twists and turns these remaining weeks may bring, help me to remember that pregnancy is only for a season. It will not last forever.

The Best Equipment

We also pray that you will be strengthened with all his glorious power so you will have all the endurance and patience you need. May you be filled with joy, always thanking the Father. He has enabled you to share in the inheritance that belongs to his people, who live in the light.
COLOSSIANS 1:11–12 NLT

Did you know that you already have the best spiritual equipment to help get you through this pregnancy?

Paul prayed that the church in Colossae would be strengthened in the Lord. That their strength wouldn't come from within, but that it would come from our heavenly Father.

So where do you get spiritually equipped to finish this pregnancy strong? Ephesians 6:14–17 (NLT) explains: "Stand your ground, putting on the belt of truth and the body armor of God's righteousness. For shoes, put on the peace that comes from the Good News so that you will be fully prepared. In addition to all of these, hold up the shield of faith to stop the fiery arrows of the devil. Put on salvation as your helmet, and take the sword of the Spirit, which is the word of God."

Every morning when you wake up, commit to praying the armor of God over you.

Father, You have given me the best equipment to help sustain me through this pregnancy. Help me not to focus on my changing body. Help me to stay focused on You!

Strengthened by God

*"So do not fear, for I am with you; do not be dismayed,
for I am your God. I will strengthen you and help you;
I will uphold you with my righteous right hand."*
ISAIAH 41:10 NIV

Over the past twenty-one weeks you probably have noticed some drastic, perhaps dramatic, changes in your body. With a rounder belly, weight gain, and stretch marks, much of you probably feels weak. What was once a strong, more put-together body is now showing signs of wear and tear. With nineteen weeks left to go, you wonder if you'll ever look like your old self again.

Here's the good news: you will. But when you do look and feel like your old self, you won't be the same person you were before pregnancy. You will be much different. It will be hard to imagine life before this pregnancy, because life will be so much better.

In Isaiah 41, God is talking to His chosen people. People who have followed Him, doubted Him even, and yet God wants them to trust and be faithful.

As you journey through this pregnancy, you might have doubts and fears. Trust God. Remain faithful. Do your part, and God will remain faithful to you. When you are weak, He will strengthen you.

Father, help me to trust that on the other side of this pregnancy I will renew my strength in You spiritually. By Your grace I believe that I will renew my strength physically too.

Safe

The spacious, free life is from GOD, it's also protected and safe. GOD-strengthened, we're delivered from evil— when we run to him, he saves us.
PSALM 37:39–40 MSG

Bella was starting to experience Braxton Hicks contractions. This was her third pregnancy, and in her previous ones she always started having contractions around this time. But this time the contractions were already getting pretty intense—about fifteen minutes apart.

Fear started to creep in. She wondered if everything was okay, if the baby was okay. She feared that she would lose the baby, that the baby would come early, or that she would end up delivering the baby at home.

Even though Bella just met with her OB the week before, she called her OB's office and asked if she could come in.

Bella's doctor believed everything was okay. She learned this can happen and it doesn't mean there's any cause for concern.

As Bella drove home from the appointment, she turned on the radio. The announcer proceeded to read Psalm 37:39–40. In that moment, Bella chose by faith to believe that she and her baby were safe. That God was with them and would protect them.

Father, becoming pregnant is a step of faith. When my mind and flesh are filled with anxiety or fear as a result of this pregnancy, please get me back on track. Help me to trust that You know every detail of this pregnancy and are strong enough to pull me through.

Stronger and Stronger

*When He prepared the heavens, I was there, when He
drew a circle on the face of the deep, when
He established the clouds above, when He
strengthened the fountains of the deep.*
PROVERBS 8:27–28 NKJV

If you think back over the past five to ten years, how have you
changed? In what ways have your faith and relationship with
the Lord strengthened? Often you might notice that before
you felt stronger in life, you had to peak. From an athlete's perspective, you had to max out your training to the point where
you had nothing left to give. You became tired, weak, perhaps
vulnerable, and almost crossed that fine line of injuring yourself.

As an athlete then starts to rest, you might have noticed
strength was rising up in you. Something was resurrecting inside
of you. And pretty soon that resurrection birthed something
new in your walk with the Lord.

All of these principles hold true during pregnancy. You
might feel weak now or in the weeks ahead, but trust you are
actually getting stronger.

---

*Lord, I trust that as a mommy-to-be I'm not only going
to give birth to a baby but also going to get to
see You strengthen my relationship with You! Help me
to hold on to You and Your Word, trusting with faith.*

Beautify the House

Blessed be the LORD God of our fathers, which hath put such a thing as this in the king's heart, to beautify the house of the LORD which is in Jerusalem: and hath extended mercy unto me before the king, and his counsellors, and before all the king's mighty princes. And I was strengthened as the hand of the LORD my God was upon me, and I gathered together out of Israel chief men to go up with me.
EZRA 7:27–28 KJV

While you still have a few weeks before your third trimester begins, you might be starting to think about the baby's nursery.

Now is a great time to start preparing and decorating the baby's room, especially if your nesting instinct has kicked in. Prior to the next trimester you might feel like you have some energy and mobility too.

As you consider the nursery, take some time to pray over the room. Meditate on Proverbs 14:26 (KJV): "In the fear of the LORD is strong confidence: and his children shall have a place of refuge." Pray for the baby's temperament, their personality, the days and nights that you will spend with them in this room. Ask the Holy Spirit to make it a refuge.

Father, I need Your Spirit to fill my baby's room with a spirit of peace. Show me how to prepare for this baby. May they be filled with Your strength and comfort within the walls of their bedroom.

Pray and Prepare

Then I told them of the hand of my God which was upon me for good, and also the words that the king had spoken to me. And they said, Let us rise up and build! So they strengthened their hands for the good work.
NEHEMIAH 2:18 AMPC

At a little over halfway until D-day, now is a great time to pray and prepare for the baby's nursery. If this is your first baby, you might also start creating a baby registry so that if people want to gift you or the baby, they know what you need.

Here are some ideas to consider as you pray and prepare for the arrival of your baby:

- Do I plan to find out the gender or not?

- What colors and themes do I want the baby's room to have?

- How do I want to express God's love for this child in this room?

- How do I want to express the love I have for this baby in this room?

Most importantly, pray over these decisions. Remember that you and your baby will be spending a lot of time in this room. So you want it to feel like a safe and enjoyable place, filled with love.

Father, help me to find creative ways to welcome this precious little baby into my home. Thank You for this gift. And thank You for the gifts You will bless our family with as a result of this new addition.

WEEK 22

♡

Valued

You and your baby continue
to get bigger. If you have any
additional ultrasound scans done,
you're going to value just how much
your baby is already starting to
look like a newborn.

Fruitful Field

*Until the Spirit is poured upon us from on high, and the
wilderness becomes a fruitful field, and the fruitful field is
valued as a forest. Then justice will dwell in the wilderness,
and righteousness (moral and spiritual rectitude in every
area and relation) will abide in the fruitful field.*

Isaiah 32:15–16 AMPC

As a young girl, Nicole always wanted to get married and
have a lot of children. She would play house with friends, and
they would talk about having more than four children. Some of
them would be twins, one boy, one girl. One would be named
Josephine and the other Joseph.

Reality set in, and so did life's daily responsibilities. Nicole
was now thirty-eight, married with three children. She figured
that, because of her age, maybe it was time for her to stop
having children. She and her husband committed to pray about
it. Sure enough, they got pregnant. . .with twins!

Nicole was excited but also anxious. How would they be
able to afford two more children? Until an old childhood friend
reminded Nicole of how they'd played growing up.

"Remember, Nicole, you always wanted to have twins!"

Now, closing in on forty years old, Nicole would see a
dream become reality.

"The Lord wants to make you a fruitful field. A fruitful home.
What a blessing, Nicole!" one friend at moms' group said to her.

---

*Father, no matter how many babies You want me to have,
help me to value life and to trust that You will provide for us.*

Highly Valued

"As surely as I valued your life today, so may the
Lord value my life and deliver me from all trouble."
Then Saul said to David, "May you be blessed, David
my son; you will do great things and surely triumph."
So David went on his way, and Saul returned home.
1 Samuel 26:24–25 niv

Saul and David had an interesting relationship. At times they were like mentor and mentee. Other times they were like oil and water. God's grace intervened in both of their lives. Enough for them to care more about how God valued the other than how they might have valued each other.

As a mommy-to-be, you might understand this sort of a relationship dynamic. Perhaps not of the same person, but maybe you know what it's like to be mentored or to mentor someone else. Maybe you know what it's like to try to have a relationship with someone who just rubs you the wrong way, but you choose to love them. No matter what you or the other person thinks, God values you!

The same holds true for your precious baby. No matter what, God values your baby.

Take some time today to pray for your baby. That God would lead you, and them, toward people who will value you both because they see you as God's children.

Father, watch over this baby's life. Guide them
to interact with others who will love and care for
them the way I desire, and the way that You desire.

Priceless

David went and comforted his wife Bathsheba.
And when he slept with her, they conceived a son.
When he was born they named him Solomon. God had a
special love for him and sent word by Nathan the prophet
that God wanted him named Jedidiah (God's Beloved).
2 SAMUEL 12:24–25 MSG

Avery led a moms' group at her daughter's church preschool. The preschool director learned that there was a new pregnancy in the church. The family was in a bit of a challenging situation though. They had just moved to the area because the wife's husband was in the military. The family didn't know anyone and had no family close by.

Avery was able to reach out to this mom and invited her to the moms' group. They learned that she was twenty-two weeks pregnant and in need of some maternity clothes; this was her first baby.

Avery led the moms' group in gathering maternity clothes as well as baby items. The mom, weary from the recent move and pregnancy, felt very supported and affirmed by the women.

Consider a time when you saw God meet a big need in your life. Praise Him for it, let Him know what you need, and consider ways you might be able to value other moms.

Lord, thank You for meeting all of my needs during this pregnancy. Thank You for the family, friends, acquaintances, and medical staff who value this precious life.

More Than Weight

*And if a man shall sanctify unto the LORD some part of
a field of his possession, then thy estimation shall be
according to the seed thereof: an homer of barley
seed shall be valued at fifty shekels of silver.*
LEVITICUS 27:16 KJV

Lacey was pregnant with her first child. Her first trimester was hard. She felt sick most of the time. She even lost some weight as a result of morning sickness and food aversions.

Just as Lacey started to feel like she had some energy to get out of the house, she noticed other symptoms emerging. She went to her prenatal appointment and learned she had gained twenty-five pounds. Only a little over halfway to delivery day, she wondered how much more weight she would gain.

Fortunately, Lacey and her husband were members of a church that had a moms' group. She decided to start attending the group and found great comfort in knowing other moms struggled with their weight gain during pregnancy.

The book of Leviticus reminds readers about the old law, the law that was adhered to religiously for the cleansing of sins. The New Testament provides hope and an assurance of God's love no matter what! So remember that no matter how much weight you might gain during this pregnancy, God still values you!

---

*God, thank You for loving me no matter how much
I weigh during pregnancy. Help me to be gracious
with myself and see myself the way You do.*

Chosen

"Isn't Israel a valued servant, born into a family with place and position? So how did she end up a piece of meat fought over by snarling and roaring lions? There's nothing left of her but a few old bones, her towns trashed and deserted. Egyptians from the cities of Memphis and Tahpanhes have broken your skulls. And why do you think all this has happened? Isn't it because you walked out on your God just as he was beginning to lead you in the right way?"
JEREMIAH 2:14–17 MSG

God used the prophet Jeremiah to speak into the lives of God's chosen people. God chose Israel to be set apart as a holy nation. When sin entered the scene, God still valued the people He created.

During this pregnancy, you might experience moments when you wonder where God is in all of this. Between the weight gain, sleep deprivation, and a body that feels run down and worn out, you might wonder when you will ever feel like yourself again.

Remember you are chosen, loved, and redeemed. God places a high value on you. Just when it starts to get really hard as a mommy-to-be, it's tempting to despair. But when pregnancy gets hard, that's God beginning to do an awesome work in you!

Father, please give me eyes to see that You are doing an awesome work in me. When I'm tempted to give up, help me to run this mommy-to-be race of faith well.

Welcoming Words

*For they loved the approval and the praise and the
glory that come from men (instead of and) more than
the glory that comes from God. (They valued their
credit with men more than their credit with God.)*
JOHN 12:43 AMPC

John's message resonated with many people, including a
mommy-to-be. He wrote about how Jesus performed miracles that caused many to believe and praise Him. Yet these
miracles caused some people, like the Pharisees, to fear even
acknowledging Jesus.

How many times have you enjoyed praise and affirmation
from others? How many times have you valued it more highly
than that of God's? Or how many times have you hoped for
affirmation but didn't get it?

As a mommy-to-be, you probably really appreciate it when
someone comes up to you and tells you how beautiful you look
pregnant. A compliment like this, even if it comes from someone
you don't know, is welcome to the ear—especially if it's a day
when you don't feel good or miss your pre-pregnancy body.

Take some time today to imagine what God would say to
you if He saw you. Consider doing something to celebrate your
baby bump. Perhaps take a picture of your baby bump and
use it as a way to share about what God is doing inside of you.

---

*Father, thank You for thinking of me as beautiful
and worthy enough to be a mommy-to-be.
Help me to live for Your glory and praise.*

Wise Words

*When he established the force of the wind and measured
out the waters, when he made a decree for the rain and a
path for the thunderstorm, then he looked at wisdom and
appraised it; he confirmed it and tested it. And he said to
the human race, "The fear of the Lord—that is wisdom,
and to shun evil is understanding."*

JOB 28:25–28 NIV

Rachel was looking forward to attending moms' group. One
of the mentor moms was going to be speaking to the group
about being pregnant while also managing a household filled
with young children.

Rachel was twenty-two weeks pregnant with her second
child, and she desperately wanted to be a mom who had
reverence for God. She grew up in a challenging home, where
faith wasn't an everyday activity.

The mentor mom spoke to the women about the importance
of fearing the Lord. She believed that if she could, by God's
grace, model that for her children, then they would come to
want a relationship with God.

The mentor mom also shared some personal reflections on
motherhood and parenting that Rachel really admired.

Think about the women in your life and ask God to show
you how they can mentor you in this season.

---

*Father, thank You for older women. Women who are moms
who love You and therefore have some wise words to
share with a mommy-to-be. Help me to value them
and to be humble enough to receive their words.*

WEEK 23

Cherished

Show how much you cherish your
baby by getting up and dancing,
walking, or moving. By now they
will be able to feel the motion!

Care Team

To cherish is to hold or treat as dear, to feel love for, to care for tenderly, or to nurture. You are cherished by God, and during pregnancy you are also cherished by others. As you begin week twenty-three of your pregnancy, think about all of the people who love you or have been caring for you. Here are some examples:

- Your family: This includes your husband, parents, children, nieces, nephews, and siblings.

- Medical care team: This includes a midwife, nurse practitioner, OB, or any other specialty care doctors.

- Your friends: This includes close friends, acquaintances, people you know at church, and neighbors.

- Jesus: He's been by your side all of the time.

Take some time today to journal or talk to God, or find another creative way to celebrate and pray for these people. Thank God for all of them. In the weeks ahead, ask God to show you how you might be able to honor them for all they have done for you throughout this pregnancy.

Father, thank You for cherishing me with an everlasting love. I love You! Help me to cherish You the way You want me to, especially during this pregnancy. Show me how to express my thanks and appreciation for all of the people in my life who have been caring for me.

Personal Treasure

Do this because you are a people set apart as holy to GOD, your God. GOD, your God, chose you out of all the people on Earth for himself as a cherished, personal treasure.
DEUTERONOMY 7:6 MSG

God gave Moses an important message for the Israelites. A message that conveyed how much God cared for them. He cared so much about their choices, their lifestyle, and their well-being that He cherished them. He considered them a personal treasure.

As a mommy-to-be, you might be able to understand this message as well. The baby inside of you is a personal treasure. You cherish this baby. You want the very best for this baby. You hope and pray that the rest of this pregnancy will go well, that you'll have a good delivery, and that this baby will sleep well. You pray that this baby will grow up to be a God-fearing individual.

It's through having a baby that you get a glimpse of how you are cherished by God. If you can love your baby this much, think about how much more God—whose love is completely unconditional—loves you! Now that's amazing!

Father, I can't comprehend Your ways. It is a mystery how You are forming this baby inside of me. It's a mystery just how much You love me and this baby. I will never fully understand Your ways, but I ask that You guide me to live a righteous and reverent life. A life that treasures You!

Tailored

*You hem me in behind and before, and you
lay your hand upon me. Such knowledge is too
wonderful for me, too lofty for me to attain.*

<small>PSALM 139:5–6 NIV</small>

Annabelle sat with her newfound friends at the moms' group.
She started going back to church shortly after giving birth to
her first child. That was two years ago, and now at twenty-three
weeks pregnant, she was starting to feel anxious about the new
demands being a mom of two would bring to the household.

Annabelle sat and listened as the moms' group leader
shared a devotion and talked about being cherished by God.

"As God's precious treasure, you were hemmed together
inside of your mother's womb. This hemming together, being
tailored by God, is a mystery. Even though we, as moms, have
read about the development of a baby inside of our womb,
the creation of life inside of us is still an amazing miracle."

Annabelle was reminded of growing up and going to church
from time to time with her grandparents. Her grandma would
often tell her about how much God cherished her.

In her heart, Annabelle decided it was time to have a real
relationship with God.

---

*Father, You have always cherished me. Even when I was
inside of my mother's womb, You loved me! Even if, at times,
I have felt unloved by others, You still nurture me. Help me to
cherish You and this baby. Thank You for knitting us together.*

Heeding

*He declares His word to Jacob, His statutes and His ordinances
to Israel. He has not dealt so with any (other) nation; they have
not known (understood, appreciated, given heed to, and
cherished) His ordinances. Praise the Lord! (Hallelujah!)*
PSALM 147:19–20 AMPC

As Annabelle listened intently to the group leader at the moms'
group, she had an epiphany. All along, since the moment she
was conceived inside of her mother's womb, God had cherished her. From the moment her baby was conceived, God
cherished this little one. But did Annabelle really cherish God?
Was she serious about her faith? How did she want to raise
her children in the faith? Like a tornado, all of these questions
started to swirl around in Annabelle's mind, creating a bit of
tension in her heart and causing her to break into a sweat.

Annabelle decided to talk with the leader about the status
of her heart and mind. Through that conversation, Annabelle
realized it was time to take seriously what her grandparents tried
to model for her growing up. Her grandparents had planted
some seeds of faith in her after her parents got divorced.

Annabelle knew what it was like to not see parents cherish
each other. At times, she didn't feel like they cherished her
either. Annabelle knew her grandparents did though. They
were like second parents to her.

*Father, I want to heed Your Word and instructions for life.
Help me to be a mommy-to-be who lives out her faith.*

Grace-Filled Gaps

*Then our sons in their youth will be like
well-nurtured plants, and our daughters
will be like pillars carved to adorn a palace.*
PSALM 144:12 NIV

"Annabelle, even though you didn't always feel cherished by your parents, God put some awesome grandparents into your life to help nurture the most important relationship you'll ever have!" Lesley, the group leader, encouraged Annabelle.

"Really? I thought the most important relationship I'll ever have is with my parents. To be honest, that has been a challenging relationship at times," Annabelle said.

"It's hard to fully understand on this side of heaven, but for you to put your faith in Jesus Christ, to accept Him into your life, to ask for His forgiveness, and to start a relationship with Him. . .that's the most important thing!" Lesley said with tears trickling down her face.

"Lesley, I want that. I'm a mom with another on the way, and I need Jesus. Being a mom is so hard. Being a mom with another on the way is exhausting. I struggle so much with what I didn't have from my parents, and yet what I want to be. I'm left feeling guilty for where I fall short."

"Annabelle, God's grace fills in the gaps. I've seen God do it for so many of the moms at our church. He can do it for you!"

*Father, help me to trust that Your grace will fill
in the gaps where I fall short as a mommy-to-be.*

Cherished by Your Mother

*I give you sound learning, so do not forsake
my teaching. For I too was a son to my father,
still tender, and cherished by my mother.*
PROVERBS 4:2–3 NIV

The moms' group leader shared with Annabelle about her childhood, accepting Christ into her life, and some of the challenges she endured with her birth parents.

"It's a process. At times it can be messy, Annabelle, but at times it is such a blessing. I wouldn't trade any of it though. I have such a deep relationship with Christ that no one can ever take away. I cherish Jesus, and I know He cherishes me."

"But will I ever feel like my mom and dad cherished me? Do you, today, ever feel like yours do?" Annabelle questioned.

"There are seasons where I see them express it more than others. I've found peace about the fact that we're all imperfect human beings. This also means that our parenting, as hard as we may try, will not be perfect. But Jesus loves me more than anyone I know. I have a peace about that now. But it took me a long time to get there."

As a mommy-to-be, take some time today to reflect on your relationship with your mom.

---

*Father, I haven't been a perfect child and my parents
aren't perfect parents. I thank You for them though.
Thank You for Your grace that has filled in the
gaps where we've all fallen short.*

Flaws and Fumbles

*If I had cherished sin in my heart, the Lord would not
have listened; but God has surely listened and has
heard my prayer. Praise be to God, who has not
rejected my prayer or withheld his love from me!*
PSALM 66:18–20 NIV

Annabelle started to cry. She wanted to have peace about
who she was as a mom and the relationship she had with her
mom. She wanted grace over her parenting flaws and fumbles.

"Annabelle, would you like to say the sinner's prayer with
me?" the moms' group leader asked her.

With tears streaming down her face, Annabelle nodded
yes. The two closed their eyes, bowed their heads, and said,
"God, I'm a sinner. I have fallen short numerous times, in numerous relationships. I have not cherished You the way You
have designed and desired of me. I'm broken, and I need
Your forgiveness. I ask for Your forgiveness. I invite You into
my life. Please cleanse me of all my sins. Thank You for dying
on the cross so that I may have eternal life with You. In Jesus'
name I pray. Amen."

Afterward, the two hugged and cried. They held hands
and smiled. This was a great day because all of Annabelle's
flaws were as white as snow.

---

*Father, I recommit my life to You. I ask for Your
forgiveness for the times I've fallen short as a
mommy-to-be. I invite You into my life as a mom.*

WEEK 24

Restored

If your belly feels like the size of a ball, you're right! According to medical advisors, your uterus is now the size of a soccer ball.

Significant Charge

I do wish, brother, that I may have some benefit from
you in the Lord; refresh my heart in Christ. Confident of
your obedience, I write to you, knowing that you will do
even more than I ask. And one thing more: Prepare
a guest room for me, because I hope to be restored
to you in answer to your prayers.
PHILEMON 1:20–22 NIV

The apostle Paul wrote a message, really a charge, to Philemon. He urged him to love others so that the love of Christ could shine through Philemon.

The calling of mommy-to-be bears the same significant charge: to love as Christ loves. Why? Because through the act of showing Christ's love and character, you have an opportunity to help restore a child back to their true Creator, God. Loving others while being a mommy-to-be isn't easy. You're carrying around precious cargo and sometimes in need of love and care from others too. It's not easy when you don't feel like loving others. But most of the time love isn't a feeling. It's a choice.

If something is restored, it is brought back into existence or use; reestablished. Today, pray that as a mommy-to-be you will have many opportunities to witness to others even in an uncomfortable state.

Father, please give me divine opportunities
to share Your love with those I interact with.

Strong Refuge

By thee have I been holden up from the womb:
thou art he that took me out of my mother's bowels:
my praise shall be continually of thee. I am as a
wonder unto many; but thou art my strong refuge.
PSALM 71:6–7 KJV

Jamie was twenty-four weeks pregnant with her first child when she experienced a series of several intense contractions that suddenly disappeared. She called her OB's office, and her husband was able to take her in to see the doctor.

After a thorough examination, Jamie's doctor didn't find anything wrong.

"I recommend that you take it easy for the next few days. Try not to do anything more than you need to. Unless anything changes, please come back and see me in forty-eight hours," her doctor concluded.

Puzzled and perplexed, Jamie and her husband left the clinic. As they sat in the car, they laid their hands over Jamie's baby bump and began to pray.

"Father God, we believe that You are the Creator and Sustainer of life. Please hold on to this baby a bit longer. Keep him or her inside; help him or her to grow and to develop well. This is our first pregnancy and we don't know what we're doing, God. Be our strong refuge."

Two days later, Jamie was doing well and the intense contractions ceased.

Father, during this pregnancy, please restore
my faith back to You when I feel vulnerable.

Check Your Focus

And behold, a certain lawyer stood up and tested Him, saying,
"Teacher, what shall I do to inherit eternal life?" He said to
him, "What is written in the law? What is your reading of it?"
So he answered and said, " 'You shall love the Lord your God
with all your heart, with all your soul, with all your strength,
and with all your mind,' and 'your neighbor as yourself.' "
Luke 10:25–27 NKJV

As a mommy-to-be, how do you feel like you're flourishing when there's so much change going on inside of your body, as well as on the outside?

In the parable of the Good Samaritan, Jesus answers the question of how to flourish in this life so that you can have eternal life. He quotes Deuteronomy 6:5 (NIV), which says: " Love the Lord your God with all your heart and with all your soul and with all your strength."

In the weeks ahead, how do you maintain a sense of vigor for the Lord? By focusing on loving the Lord with all of your heart, soul, and strength. Jesus also adds in the New Testament to love your neighbor as yourself.

So when you have a mommy-to-be moment and you feel like you're failing more than flourishing, check your focus.

Father, I desire to stay focused on You. Give me Your
strength to love You with all that I have, and to love others.

Mighty Miracles

*O God, you have taught me from my earliest childhood,
and I constantly tell others about the wonderful things you
do. Now that I am old and gray, do not abandon me,
O God. Let me proclaim your power to this new generation,
your mighty miracles to all who come after me.*
PSALM 71:17–18 NLT

At twenty-four weeks pregnant, Kelly committed to speak at a moms' group about God's miracles. For one, this subject hit close to home for her. She had two kids in her early thirties, and now just a couple of years away from turning forty, she found herself pregnant with her third child. She and her husband had often talked about having one more child if they could. But still this pregnancy was a surprise.

As Kelly prepared for the message, she found herself relying heavily on the Lord's grace and strength. It was hard for her to stand on her feet for more than fifteen minutes without getting tired, let alone speaking for more than thirty minutes. Kelly decided to stick to her commitment and trust that somehow she would get to experience God's grace—perhaps even a mighty miracle at her age.

*God, as I reflect on this pregnancy, I thank You for
helping me do things I didn't think I could do because
I'm pregnant. Through those experiences, I got to
witness Your grace and strength work in and through
me. Thank You for those mighty miracles!*

Home in God

Surely or only goodness, mercy, and unfailing love shall follow me all the days of my life, and through the length of my days the house of the Lord (and His presence) shall be my dwelling place.
PSALM 23:6 AMPC

David wrote Psalm 23, which portrays God as a restorer. David called the Lord his Shepherd.

A shepherd is a person who oversees a group of sheep. They help guide the sheep, watching over and protecting them. They look out for their best interest. When one goes astray out of the whole group, the shepherd will help that one lonely sheep find its way back to the group. The shepherd helps to restore the sheep and the community of sheep.

Only God has the power and strength to restore you. It's through His grace and mercy that you can find hope, life, and forgiveness. It's through His love that you can receive adoption into His family.

As you prepare to embark on the last month of the second trimester, consider how you have found home in God. Take some time today to celebrate how God's love has restored your life as a mommy-to-be.

God, You are an awesome Father! Though I try so hard to make my home a good place to be, ultimately You are home. Help me to shower my baby with the kind of love that they need and that You desire for me to share with them.

A Double Portion

After Job had interceded for his friends, GOD restored his
fortune—and then doubled it! All his brothers and sisters
and friends came to his house and celebrated. They told
him how sorry they were, and consoled him for all the
trouble GOD had brought him. Each of them brought
generous housewarming gifts.
JOB 42:10–11 MSG

Whitney was already starting to deal with leg cramps and
heartburn. At twenty-four weeks, she was feeling tired. However,
she was also very grateful. It took her and her husband several
attempts to get pregnant for the first time. They walked through
two miscarriages. Now she was pregnant with twins!

Whitney was a bit astounded by the Lord's goodness
though. As she shared with some women at the moms' group
at church, she felt like the Lord was blessing them with twins
out of the loss of their other two babies.

Furthermore, Whitney was starting to feel a bit overwhelmed.
She created a baby registry but wasn't sure if she should ask
for double the amount of everything. One mom encouraged
Whitney by telling her that God would supply everything they
needed to have for the twins. His grace was big enough to fill
in the gap where she might miss an item.

Abba, thank You for Your grace that blankets my
mommy-to-be moments. I'm in awe of Your grace
and mercy that so gently captivates me. Help me
to have eyes to see how You're blessing me.

A Little Child

Then he went down and dipped himself seven times in the Jordan, as the man of God had said, and his flesh was restored like that of a little child, and he was clean.
2 Kings 5:14 AMPC

While holding an egg bake, Ruthie waddled her way into moms' group. Smiling ear to ear, she placed the egg bake near the other food items and found a place to sit. One of the leaders came up to her and asked how she was doing.

"Our prayers were answered! Remember two weeks ago when you prayed for me and the baby? There were some concerns about the baby's kidneys, and yesterday's ultrasound showed there's nothing to worry about! The fluid that had been inside the kidneys is now gone!"

"That's wonderful news, Ruthie! Can you share that with the other moms today so that they might be encouraged? We'd like to continue to pray for you too."

Ruthie was so grateful as she shared the news with the whole group. Her testimony of God restoring her baby's kidneys encouraged the other moms. It inspired one of the leaders to provide a time of corporate and individual prayer.

Father, thank You for restoring my life. When I have felt anxious as a mommy-to-be, thank You for those who have been so gracious to have compassion and pray for me and this little one. Help me to pray for others in their time of need.

WEEK 25

Renewed

You might start to feel renewed as you regain some energy. In just a few more weeks you will start the third trimester.

One Thing

*Put on your new nature, and be renewed as you learn to
know your Creator and become like him. In this new life,
it doesn't matter if you are a Jew or a Gentile, circumcised
or uncircumcised, barbaric, uncivilized, slave, or free.
Christ is all that matters, and he lives in all of us.*

COLOSSIANS 3:10–11 NLT

The apostle Paul wrote a letter to Christians in Colossae about what it meant to live for Christ. He urged them to live a new life, a transformed life, that focused on one thing. What was this one thing? Christ. To Paul, Christ was all that mattered. His death and resurrection were the hallmark for forgiveness and eternal life. His sacrifice was the one thing that would save and renew a person's life.

As a mommy-to-be, putting Christ at the center of this high calling will renew you. Focusing on your relationship with Christ won't be taxing or time-consuming. Instead it will provide strength when you feel weary. It will give you grace-filled eyes to see that you can get things done, you can find rest and peace during sleepless nights.

Above all else, think about how God has renewed you in unexpected ways in the past few weeks. Praise Him for it.

---

*Father, as this pregnancy progresses, continue to pour out
Your Spirit within me. I desire to overflow with Your goodness
even when I don't have the strength or ability on my own.*

Rejoice with Joy

*The Lord your God is in the midst of you, a Mighty One,
a Savior (Who saves)! He will rejoice over you with joy;
He will rest (in silent satisfaction) and in His love He will be
silent and make no mention (of past sins, or even recall
them); He will exult over you with singing.*
ZEPHANIAH 3:17 AMPC

McKenzie was sitting at the back of the church community room. The nearly full table at the moms' group was striking up a deep, thought-provoking discussion about motherhood. The five women sitting at the table all understood McKenzie's stage of life—her joys and struggles.

McKenzie's past had produced so much pain that she almost didn't want to have children. Past sins caused her faith to waver.

But there was also joy. They read Zephaniah 3:17, which reminded the women that no matter where they were in their journey of motherhood—whether a mommy-to-be or a soon-to-be empty-nester—God would forgive, restore, and renew their relationships.

McKenzie was so grateful for these women who shared their joys and struggles of motherhood. As a first-time mommy-to-be, she felt assurance that God was with her and that He would continue to carry her through this pregnancy.

---

*Father, whether this is my first time, second time,
third time, or more, thank You for helping me take
the step of faith in becoming a mommy-to-be.
I give You the praise, honor, and glory.*

The Pregnancy Process

Therefore, I urge you, brothers and sisters, in view of God's mercy, to offer your bodies as a living sacrifice, holy and pleasing to God—this is your true and proper worship. Do not conform to the pattern of this world, but be transformed by the renewing of your mind. Then you will be able to test and approve what God's will is—his good, pleasing and perfect will.
ROMANS 12:1–2 NIV

By now as a mommy-to-be, you probably understand what it means to offer your body as a living sacrifice. For the past twenty-five weeks you have endured surrendering your body to the process of pregnancy.

So how do you find renewal while pregnant? How do you become restored and replenished? By focusing on what's ahead. A few months from now you will be holding a little baby. In several more months you will get to witness a first smile or giggle. A year from now, you might be sleeping a little bit better, and your child might start taking their first steps. In turn, you will be a new person. Different, yes. Better? Absolutely! All because of laying down your life for another.

Father, please give me a fresh vision for what's ahead as a mommy-to-be. Help me not to lose sight of You along the way and how You're renewing me throughout the pregnancy process.

God Is Your God

This very day GOD, your God, commands you to follow
these rules and regulations, to live them out with everything
you have in you. You've renewed your vows today that
GOD is your God, that you'll live the way he shows you;
do what he tells you in the rules, regulations,
and commandments; and listen obediently to him.
DEUTERONOMY 26:16–17 MSG

The book of Deuteronomy was a record of sermons that Moses spoke to the Israelites. In today's passage of scripture, Moses emphasized the importance of following the Lord's commands.

In the Old Testament, you will be reminded time and again of the law believers had to adhere to in order to be forgiven by God. Because Jesus Christ died, we don't have to adhere to such a strict law. So why is what Moses said then pertinent to you today as a mommy-to-be?

Because if you love the Lord your God with all of your heart, soul, and strength, and love your neighbor as yourself (Deuteronomy 6:5; Mark 12:30–31), you will experience a flourishing life. Even when you're tired, weary, and perplexed by the daily demands of being a mommy-to-be, you will experience a renewed sense of faith. You will receive a fresh perspective on your role as mommy.

Father, I desire to be set apart. Show me Your ways so
that I might walk in them fully. When You call me to
do something, give me the strength to obey You.

Point to God with Praise

Bless the LORD, O my soul: and all that is within me,
bless his holy name. Bless the LORD, O my soul, and forget
not all his benefits: who forgiveth all thine iniquities; who
healeth all thy diseases; who redeemeth thy life from
destruction; who crowneth thee with lovingkindness and
tender mercies; who satisfieth thy mouth with good things;
so that thy youth is renewed like the eagle's.
PSALM 103:1–5 KJV

McKenzie was thinking back on the conversation she had with the moms at her church's moms' group. She appreciated their different stages of life and the insight they brought to the group. Their perspective gave her some peace of mind. Their stories renewed her vision for the weeks ahead until delivery.

McKenzie took some time to open her Bible and read some of the Psalms. This passage in Psalm 103 stood out to her. She really liked how it mentioned being renewed like the eagles. Why? Because an eagle symbolizes strength and grace—two things she desired to experience more and more in the weeks ahead.

During your pregnancy, reflect on a time you felt like you were soaring. Maybe it was when you first found out you were pregnant, or maybe it was when you had a good night's sleep. Whatever it was, take some time to praise God for it.

Father, give me moments when You renew
my faith. Moments that allow me to point
to You with praise during this pregnancy.

Day by Day

*Therefore we do not lose heart. Even though
our outward man is perishing, yet the inward
man is being renewed day by day.*
2 CORINTHIANS 4:16 NKJV

"I feel like I'm losing so much of myself. One day I forget things. The next day I step on the scale and can't believe I've already gained thirty pounds," Olivia shared with the women at the moms' group she attended.

"I know exactly how you feel, Olivia," one of her tablemates agreed. "When I was in my teens I dreamed of being a mom. I couldn't wait to be pregnant. Now here I am. I'm exhausted, uncomfortable. Jenny, how do you do it with four kids?"

Jenny looked at each mom. Some tears welled up underneath her lower eyelids.

"Ladies, all I can say is that it's God's grace that carried me through all four of my pregnancies. It has been God's grace in raising my children. And it has gone way too fast. There's a part of me that misses the stage of life you're now in," Jenny said. "Ladies, try to take it one day at a time. You might feel like you're wasting away. The reality is you are growing stronger in your relationship with God than you ever have before."

---

*Father, use this pregnancy to renew my faith
in You. Though I feel like I'm wasting away,
I trust that I'm growing stronger in You.*

A New Nature

Jenny continued to encourage the mommies-to-be sitting at her table.

"I just want my old body back," Olivia said. "I realize that I will get my body back eventually, but it will be completely different. Won't it?" she asked Jenny and the other moms.

"Yes, Olivia, your body will be different. But if you stay focused on the Lord, you will find that in a year or two you will have a renewed spirit. That's far more important than your outward appearance," Noel, one of the mentor moms, said.

"That sounds easier said than done," one of the mommies-to-be protested.

"Yes, it is. But start praying. And I'll be praying for you all too, that a year from now you will have much to praise God for. Just you wait and see!"

"I agree with Noel. I'm going to pray for you all too," encouraged Jenny. "In fact, I will pray for you right now and for all of us, that God will renew our minds."

Father, when it feels like my hormones are raging and taking over my body and mind, please help me to trust You. Lord, renew my mind and body. When I look back on this pregnancy, I want to have much to praise You for.

WEEK 26

♡

Baptized

As you gear up for the third trimester,
your baby is practicing breathing by
inhaling and exhaling amniotic fluid.

Declare

For you will be His witness unto all men of everything that you have seen and heard. And now, why do you delay? Rise and be baptized, and by calling upon His name, wash away your sins.
ACTS 22:15–16 AMPC

Why is being baptized so important to the apostle Paul, and to many other Christians today? Baptism is a declaration of your faith. It's a public testimony of the former life you're choosing to leave behind, in order to live for and obey Jesus Christ. It is a way of sharing with those in your Christian community that you want to be held accountable to God's standards and principles.

As a mommy-to-be, you might be thinking about how to declare your faith as a parent to your baby. Depending on your convictions, you might decide to get your baby baptized or dedicated to the Lord. This decision is sometimes influenced by what you experienced as a child. So take some time today to pray about what you might like to do for your baby. Here are some things to consider:

- How do you want to celebrate your child's birth within your church community?
- How do you want to support your child as they grow up in the faith?

Father, the decision to have my baby baptized or dedicated to You is a big one. I don't want to take it lightly! Show me how You want me to celebrate and support this child.

Being Baptized

After this, Jesus and his disciples went out into the Judean countryside, where he spent some time with them, and baptized. Now John also was baptizing at Aenon near Salim, because there was plenty of water, and people were coming and being baptized.

JOHN 3:22–23 NIV

What does it mean to be baptized? Usually someone taking part in the sacrament of baptism is immersed in water or sprinkled with water. It is a representation of spiritual death and resurrection to new life in Christ.

Were you baptized or dedicated as a baby? If not, did you get baptized later in life? Or have you not been baptized at all?

Now that you're a mommy-to-be, these are some important faith questions to ask yourself. You don't need to have all of the answers, but it's wise to prayerfully consider and seek the Lord's guidance on how to follow through with baptism or a dedication. This is an important step not just for your baby, but for you as a parent. It's an opportunity to publicly declare your desire to raise this baby with Christian values.

If you haven't been baptized, also be prayerful about how you might be able to do so. God loves you and wants to celebrate your commitment to Him.

Father, lead and guide me on the right path toward raising this baby. Show me how to dedicate this baby so that they are under Your authority and supported by other Christians.

A Changed, Cleansed Life

John dressed in a camel-hair habit tied at the waist by a leather strap. He lived on a diet of locusts and wild field honey. People poured out of Jerusalem, Judea, and the Jordanian countryside to hear and see him in action. There at the Jordan River those who came to confess their sins were baptized into a changed life.

MATTHEW 3:4–6 MSG

Many had come to be baptized by John the Baptist. They heard about the life-changing message of Jesus Christ. They felt led to publicly declare their new birth and enter into a new way of life by declaring themselves sinners who were saved and forgiven by the grace of God.

To be baptized is to be cleansed spiritually. To wash away the old and make way for the new. As a mommy-to-be, your baptism allows for you to be made clean and new. At that moment of baptism, all is washed away.

If you have been baptized and you can remember when that public declaration occurred, think back to that day. How did you feel before you were immersed in water? How did you feel afterward?

As a mommy-to-be, maybe take a bath or go into a pool. Re-create this act of submerging yourself in water as a reminder that every day you are cleansed by God's grace and mercy.

Father, thank You for reminding me that my baptism was just the beginning of a daily reminder that You have changed and cleansed my life!

Descending and Ascending

When He had been baptized, Jesus came up immediately from the water; and behold, the heavens were opened to Him, and He saw the Spirit of God descending like a dove and alighting upon Him. And suddenly a voice came from heaven, saying, "This is My beloved Son, in whom I am well pleased."
MATTHEW 3:16–17 NKJV

Kathy was talking at the moms' group about being baptized. She was baptized as an infant, so she didn't remember the milestone. However, she had pictures, a certificate, and even her infant baptism gown. As an adult she thought about getting baptized again, but life caught up to her. Now, at twenty-six weeks pregnant, she wondered what to do.

"As a mommy-to-be, I really didn't feel a sense of urgency about what to do until now. With our first child on the way, I'm really thinking through how to dedicate their life. Should I baptize them when they are little or when they are older and can make the decision for themselves?"

"Kathy, if you feel like you need to talk with someone about it, you can certainly ask us or one of the pastors on staff. Just know that you can take your time in making this decision," one of the moms encouraged her.

Father, help me to be humble enough to talk to others about baptism. As a mommy-to-be, show me the next steps I can take to continually dedicate my life to You.

Share the Spirit

The human body has many parts, but the many parts make up one whole body. So it is with the body of Christ. Some of us are Jews, some are Gentiles, some are slaves, and some are free. But we have all been baptized into one body by one Spirit, and we all share the same Spirit.

1 CORINTHIANS 12:12–13 NLT

The apostle Paul recognized the importance of being a part of one body with many parts. The body is the church, and the many parts are the believers who make up the church. What is the common denominator? Jesus.

As a mommy-to-be, you might have become quickly aware of other women around you who are in the same stage of life as you. Some might be pregnant for their first, second, or third time. You all have different backgrounds and experiences that may have brought you together. And if you are able to be among a community of Christian moms, you get to share in the Spirit of Christ.

Take some time today to thank God for putting other moms in your life who are going through the same things you are. Women who don't have it all together, but at the center of your relationship is Christ.

Lord, You're awesome! I praise You for putting other pregnant moms into my life so that we don't have to go through this calling alone.

Put on Christ

*For ye are all the children of God by faith in
Christ Jesus. For as many of you as have been
baptized into Christ have put on Christ.*
GALATIANS 3:26–27 KJV

Jasmine and some friends at the church moms' group started
talking about baptism. The conversation was spurred on by the
speaker who came to their group that morning.

"Ladies, I want you to think about your baptism. When was
it? Were you an infant, or were you older? What does baptism
mean to you as a mom and to your family?" The speaker asked
the women to discuss these things at their tables.

All of these questions were great conversation starters.
Jasmine was surprised to hear so many different perspectives
on baptism at her table. For her, she was baptized as an infant,
but in college she decided to get baptized again. Jasmine felt
like she had a better understanding of baptism as an adult. But
as a mommy-to-be, she wasn't sure what to do for her baby.

She asked the other moms for some perspective. "Do I
dedicate my baby and then let them make the decision later
in life?"

If you were baptized as an infant or an adult, thank God
for allowing you to be a child of His.

---

*Father, earnestly I seek Your guidance for
my baby's life. I pray this child will come
to know You at a young age. As their mom,
guide me in how to lead them toward baptism.*

Resurrection Moments

*When you came to Christ, you were "circumcised," but
not by a physical procedure. Christ performed a spiritual
circumcision—the cutting away of your sinful nature. For you
were buried with Christ when you were baptized. And with
him you were raised to new life because you trusted the
mighty power of God, who raised Christ from the dead.*
COLOSSIANS 2:11–12 NLT

From Paul's perspective, being baptized was a symbolic resurrection in the life of a believer. When a person is submerged
in water, it reflects a burial of the old self and sins. As a person
emerges from the water, it reflects a resurrection of new life.

As a mommy-to-be, you may have already experienced
several resurrection moments. Moments when you've had to
die to self, let go, or lay something down for the sake of your
baby. Perhaps it has been your diet, exercise, sleep, or clothes.
Or maybe throughout these past twenty-six weeks, you have
had to depend on the Lord more than you ever have before.

On the other side of pregnancy will come a resurrection.
New life will come out of you, and you will enter into a new
season of life.

---

*Father, thank You that I can partner with
You in this life. Thank You for baptism and the
remembrance of what resurrection is in my own life.*

WEEK 27

♡

Appointed

As you continue to grow and prepare
for the third trimester, you might start
to notice some rapid movement or
jolting. The cause? Baby has hiccups!

Appointed by God

The word of the LORD came to me, saying, "Before I formed you in the womb I knew you, before you were born I set you apart; I appointed you as a prophet to the nations."
JEREMIAH 1:4–5 NIV

Jeremiah was a prophet. The title and job description weren't just handed to him though. He didn't interview for the job either. In fact, he didn't want it. He felt unqualified and unfit for the title. But God didn't see that. God saw promise and purpose. God saw a young man with a calling to fulfill while living on earth.

Maybe you can relate to Jeremiah. As a mommy-to-be, you might also feel unqualified and unfit for the job description. You might wish you had instructions or the chance to interview for the role. But God sees you. He has called you by name. You have been appointed by God for such a time as this to raise up the next generation of children. How awesome is that? You have the opportunity to lead, guide, and influence a little life.

While it might be helpful to have a job description, guess what? You don't need it. All you need is God. If you want instructions, seek His Word. He won't let you down.

Father, being a mommy-to-be is a high calling. Don't let me underestimate all that You have in store for me as I prepare to birth new life into this world. Help me to lean on You.

Be an Example

These things command and teach. Let no man despise thy
youth; but be thou an example of the believers, in word,
in conversation, in charity, in spirit, in faith, in purity.
1 TIMOTHY 4:11–12 KJV

Timothy was appointed by God to preach. He was a young pastor working for the church in Ephesus. His mentor was none other than the apostle Paul. Paul wrote to encourage Timothy to command and teach God's Word. Furthermore, Paul encouraged Timothy to be an example to those he interacted with. This was a high calling because Timothy was young.

As a mommy-to-be, you are young too. You're in a season of life that can be considered hard, chaotic, and tiresome. But with every obstacle comes an opportunity. What's the opportunity that you have been given during this season of life? To be an example. Even when you're tired, weary, burdened, and broken, you can still be used by God. Being a witness for Christ will look different from one day to the next. With God's strength you can do it though, and you don't have to let inexperience discourage you. You can rise above with Jesus because you're His child.

Father, as a mommy-to-be I desire to live out Your Word
in my life. I desire to be an example to my family and to
other women around me. Help me to read Your scripture
daily and to obey You. For Your glory. Amen.

High Five

And today GOD has reaffirmed that you are dearly held treasure just as he promised, a people entrusted with keeping his commandments, a people set high above all other nations that he's made, high in praise, fame, and honor: you're a people holy to GOD, your God. That's what he has promised.
DEUTERONOMY 26:18–19 MSG

Angela wanted nothing more than to be affirmed by her mom. New in the faith and pregnant with her first baby, she started attending a moms' group at her local church. She shared with the women her struggles to get pregnant. Now that she was, it surfaced a lot of emotions as she tried to reconcile with her mom and prepare to become a mom.

"God loves you, Angela. No matter what you've gone through, He accepts you. See here. Read with me Deuteronomy 26:18–19," one of the group leaders encouraged her.

"Even though you have dealt with pain, God has called you to become a mom. If you remain in His Word, Angela, you will heal and flourish."

Take some time to reflect on, and pray about, your relationship with your mom. Thank God for helping you get to a place to become a mommy-to-be and ask Him to help you in your relationships.

Father, being a mommy-to-be has caused me to reflect on the relationship I have with my own mom. Help me to be the kind of mom that You desire me to be.

The Appointed One

*Then times of refreshment will come from the presence
of the Lord, and he will again send you Jesus, your
appointed Messiah. For he must remain in heaven until
the time for the final restoration of all things, as God
promised long ago through his holy prophets.*
ACTS 3:20–21 NLT

Jesus was appointed by God to come to earth. He took on
human form and humbled Himself on a tree. There, He was
crucified. He died and was buried. On the third day He rose
again. Why did He do all of this for us? Because He loved us,
wanted us to spend eternity with Him, and wanted to fulfill the
law for the forgiveness of sins. Now you can go to Him and have
instant access to His love and forgiveness.

This is great news! It's the Gospel message that you have
access to on your best days and your worst. Even better? Jesus
will one day come again. Until that time, the human race will
go on. Babies, like the one you are carrying, are born into this
world with a calling: to proclaim this good news, to be baptized,
and to enter into a right relationship with God.

---

*Father, thank You for what You did for me and my
baby on the cross. You were appointed to do so
and I'm grateful You did. As a mommy-to-be, please
show me how to live in humble obedience to You.*

An Assignment

Withstand (the devil); be firm in faith (against his onset—rooted, established, strong, immovable, and determined), knowing that the same (identical) sufferings are appointed to your brotherhood (the whole body of Christians) throughout the world.
1 Peter 5:9 AMPC

Avery attended her twenty-seven-week prenatal appointment. This was her second pregnancy, and she could tell she was feeling very fatigued, hungry, and thirsty. Even though she had gained the same amount of weight as her first, she didn't remember feeling this way during that pregnancy.

The day before her prenatal appointment, Avery went through the standard glucose screening for gestational diabetes. As she met with her OB, there was some unexpected news.

"Avery, I'm sorry to have to tell you this, but you have gestational diabetes," her OB shared with her.

Avery felt ashamed, but her OB assured her that a few changes in her diet would help.

"Over the next few weeks, Avery, your assignment is to meet with a nutritionist. They will help you adhere to a good diet. You'll also have a few more visits and tests with me. But don't worry, you're going to be okay. This happens to many women. After they give birth the diabetes symptoms are usually gone."

Avery was concerned but prayed to God for His grace and mercy to help her in these last few weeks of pregnancy.

Father, I need Your wisdom to know what to eat and drink that is good for my body and the baby's.

Handpicked

*(The Lord) appointed the moon for the seasons;
the sun knows (the exact time of) its setting.*
PSALM 104:19 AMPC

The writer of Psalm 104 praised God. He was in awe of Him
and expressed his reverence for Him. He acknowledged that
everything has been chosen, ordained, and handpicked by
God. Every detail, including the seasons and night and day, is
fixed under God's authority.

For you and your baby, every defining detail inside of your
womb has been appointed by God. This time, this season of your
life, was predestined to cultivate, nurture, and birth your baby.

So take some time today to journal or do something else
creative to express your affirmation and affection for God and
this baby. If you have ultrasound pictures, or baby bump pictures, consider creating a special place to store them. If you
have started working on the baby's nursery, perhaps take a
few pictures that will help you remember how it looks during
this season. (Before you know it, that room won't look like a
nursery!) And maybe write out some neat milestones like how
it feels when your baby kicks, hiccups, or moves around.

---

*Father, some days this pregnancy feels so long. But when
I look back over the course of the past few months,
it has gone quickly! Thank You for handpicking me to
be a mommy-to-be for such a time as this.*

High Orders

*I appointed twelve leaders of the priests—Sherebiah,
Hashabiah, and ten other priests—to be in charge of
transporting the silver, the gold, the gold bowls, and the
other items that the king, his council, his officials, and all the
people of Israel had presented for the Temple of God.*

Ezra 8:24–25 nlt

Nicki was so excited for the moms' group. Five of the eight women on the leadership team were expecting babies. It was a lot of fun for her and the other moms to be in this season of life together. It was also reasonable to expect that since five of the moms were going to be delivering soon, change was in order for the leadership team.

"Ladies, at our next meeting we will be talking with all of you about our positions. Five of us eight will not be returning to the leadership team next year. Which means that this is an opportunity for you all to step up and lead," Nicki shared during the announcements portion of the meeting.

"Many of us have been serving this ministry for several years. We're sad to step down, but at the same time this is exciting. New moms can step into these roles. We ask that you would please pray for this ministry and how you can get involved."

---

*Father, a lot of change is in store. Help me to be
faithful to pray about my priorities and what
I need to step away from for a season.*

WEEK 28

♡

Redeemed

Congratulations! You've made
it to the third trimester!

A Good Life

*Who gave Himself on our behalf that He might
redeem us (purchase our freedom) from all iniquity
and purify for Himself a people (to be peculiarly His own,
people who are) eager and enthusiastic about (living
a life that is good and filled with) beneficial deeds.*
TITUS 2:14 AMPC

The apostle Paul wrote in Titus chapter 2 about doing good
for the sake of the Gospel. Why? Because what Jesus did on
the cross redeemed believers from the bondage of sin. Jesus'
sacrifice birthed a good life. A life filled with freedom and
forgiveness.

As a mommy-to-be, you have a ministry right in front of
you. By now your belly might be the first thing you see (or think
about), and that's a great place to start. As a child of God you
have been redeemed. Now you have an awesome opportunity
to share this same redeeming love with your baby.

So take some time to think about those who have poured
their love into you. Praise God for giving you not a perfect life,
or a condemned life, but a good life! Praise God for putting
others in your life so that they can share in the good news of
Jesus Christ.

---

*Father, thank You for giving me a good life
that started the day I accepted You into my life.
As a mommy-to-be, help me to think of creative
ways to share Your love with my baby.*

A Father

And will be a Father unto you, and ye shall be
my sons and daughters, saith the Lord Almighty.
2 CORINTHIANS 6:18 KJV

The apostle Paul warned the Christians in Corinth against idolatry. Instead he encouraged them to let their sole focus be on their heavenly Father. He reminded them that their body was a temple, and he referred to Jeremiah 32:38 when he wrote, "I will live with them and walk among them, and I will be their God, and they will be my people" (2 Corinthians 6:16 NIV).

Take some time today, or in the next few days, to think about your parents. Reflect on their attributes that you consider honorable. Praise God for them and think of a way to highlight the characteristics you're thankful for. Maybe write a letter, send them a card, or simply journal a prayer for them. Praise God for being your Father above all else, the One who loves you unconditionally. Thank God for giving you your parents, who did the best they could to love you, despite their imperfections.

Father, I'm grateful for my parents. Without them I wouldn't
be who I am today. Most of all, thank You for loving me with
an everlasting love. Thank You for meeting all of my needs.
As I prepare to parent this child, show me how I can honor
my parents and express gratitude for their love.

Redemption Legacy

Praise the Lord! How joyful are those who fear the Lord and delight in obeying his commands. Their children will be successful everywhere; an entire generation of godly people will be blessed.
PSALM 112:1–2 NLT

For you as a mommy-to-be, what Jesus did on the cross refines but also defines you. He paid for your sins on the cross. He redeemed you, paid off your debt, and bought you back. Now that He lives inside of you and you have eternal life with Him, you get to pass on this redemption legacy to your baby! How cool is that?

As your baby continues to form and grow inside of you this last trimester, consider all of their intricate details. The inner workings of their frame. Everything you have eaten and drank has gone through their body. God has been knitting them together, which is a profound mystery.

Like the baby who grows and has all they need passing through their body, you also have everything you need in Christ. The Holy Spirit fills your body to birth good works. These good works don't save you. These good works define you as being different: redeemed.

Take some time today to reflect on the godly legacy you want to instill in your baby's life.

Father, lead me along the right path. A path that helps me point to You as I prepare for the birth of this baby.

Necklaces and Tablets

My son, do not forget my law, but let your heart keep my
commands; for length of days and long life and peace they
will add to you. Let not mercy and truth forsake you; bind them
around your neck, write them on the tablet of your heart, and
so find favor and high esteem in the sight of God and man.
PROVERBS 3:1–4 NKJV

Sara was so grateful to be visiting a new moms' group. She was invited by the leaders to speak to the group about living a redeemed life with Christ. For Sara, this wasn't an easy topic. By God's grace she knew He called her to do it, and so she rested in His peace.

A key scripture for her message was Proverbs 3:1–4. For Sara, this message was a humbling one as well. At twenty-eight weeks pregnant, it was hard for her to stand up for more than half an hour at a time. She didn't exactly look the most glamorous either. But she believed she would find favor since these women were moms. She prayed they would esteem her for being so willing to minister to them.

As she spoke to the moms, Sara was reminded of cross necklaces and her baptism certificate, items that spoke to her of Christ's love and redemption in her life.

Father, this baby inside of my belly is a reminder
of Your goodness and faithfulness in my life.

Self-Absorbed

*Christ redeemed us from the curse of the law by becoming a
curse for us, for it is written: "Cursed is everyone who is hung
on a pole." He redeemed us in order that the blessing given
to Abraham might come to the Gentiles through Christ Jesus,
so that by faith we might receive the promise of the Spirit.*
GALATIANS 3:13–14 NIV

Sara shared that her cross necklace was given to her at her
baptism as an adult. The certificate had Galatians 3:13–14 on it.

"Ladies, this was a verse that nailed it for me," she shared
with the moms.

"When I read this verse at the age of twenty, I knew it was
time for me to commit my life to Christ. I knew a lot about Jesus,
but I didn't have a relationship with Him. I was so tired and worn
out from my sin. I tried so hard to do things right, but never felt
like it was enough. Then God helped me to see I didn't have
to be good enough. He redeemed me. As a mom, He says I'm
enough and so is this child. This might sound a bit self-absorbed,
ladies, but from time to time I say out loud that I am enough. It
reminds me that I am, but not because of anything I've done.
It's all because of the saving grace of what Christ did for us."

*Father, thank You that I'm truly enough.
I'm enough because of what You did on
the cross! Thank You for redeeming me!*

A Lifetime of Jubilee

"If he is not redeemed in any of these ways, he goes free in the year of Jubilee, he and his children, because the People of Israel are my servants, my servants whom I brought out of Egypt. I am GOD, your God."
LEVITICUS 25:54–55 MSG

In the Old Testament, the year of Jubilee was like a year of redemption. Any outstanding debt that was owed would be forgiven. Any slaves or prisoners would be freed. Grace, favor, and mercy would abound.

The best part about the New Testament, the Gospel message, is that you—a mommy-to-be—can experience jubilee any time of the year! Why? Because of the ransom Jesus Christ paid for you on the cross. This ransom that was paid allows for you to have complete access to God, no questions asked.

So go forth today with peace in your heart, knowing that you are a forgiven, loved, accepted, and valued daughter of Christ. Perhaps you don't always feel this way. Maybe people close to you don't always treat you as such. But God does! He loves you, pregnant and all! So go out rejoicing in this good news!

Father, no matter how I feel today, help me to rejoice with jubilee for what You did for me and this precious baby on the cross. Thank You for humbling Yourself enough to die so that I may have eternal life with You! Help me to share this jubilee with my baby.

Rescued and Redeemed

You drew near on the day I called to You; You said, Fear not.
O Lord, You have pleaded the causes of my soul (You have
managed my affairs and You have protected my person
and my rights); You have rescued and redeemed my life!
LAMENTATIONS 3:57–58 AMPC

As Sara's message to the moms' group came to a close, she needed to sit down. She had been on her feet for nearly thirty minutes. At twenty-eight weeks pregnant she was getting tired.

Sara led the women in prayer. As she did, she invited other moms there to pray the sinner's prayer with her. Assuming that not every mom in the room had accepted Christ into her life, she asked all of the women to bow their heads so she could pray. Sara then asked the women to raise their hands if it was the first time they received Christ into their life. To Sara's surprise she saw two hands raised.

Sara continued to pray, and as she did she opened her Bible to Lamentations 3:57–58 and read the words out loud. Her prayer focused on the last part of the passage: how God rescued and redeemed them.

Consider how God has rescued and redeemed you. Praise Him for it.

Father, You have rescued and redeemed me!
I don't deserve it, but You say I am! Thank You
for this precious treasure. Help me to embrace
Your redeeming message and share it with others.

WEEK 29

♡

Adored

Your baby's lungs continue to mature.
If this is your first pregnancy, you will
be working on your baby registry,
getting ready to be adored and
blessed by others with a baby shower!

All In

Jesus said unto him, Thou shalt love the Lord thy God with all thy heart, and with all thy soul, and with all thy mind. This is the first and great commandment. And the second is like unto it, Thou shalt love thy neighbour as thyself.
MATTHEW 22:37–39 KJV

Jesus was tested. Again. This time the Pharisees—experts in the law—wanted to know the greatest commandment in the Old Testament. Jesus knew the Hebrew Bible. He knew what the greatest commandment was, found in Deuteronomy 6:5 (KJV): "And thou shalt love the LORD thy God with all thine heart, and with all thy soul, and with all thy might."

As a mommy-to-be, is this commandment a reality for you? Ask the Holy Spirit to search your heart, soul, and mind. Are you all in for what God has for you? Are you all in when it comes to depending on God to continue to help you through this pregnancy and on into motherhood?

Pray and ask God to show you what it looks like to be a mommy-to-be who is all in. One who is devoted to God with all your heart, soul, and mind. One who also loves your neighbor as yourself.

Father, help me to be the mommy-to-be that You desire. Pregnancy isn't just all about me and my needs. It's also about You living in and through me, despite my weaknesses. Help me to glorify You.

Delighted

*My child, don't reject the LORD's discipline, and don't be
upset when he corrects you. For the LORD corrects those he
loves, just as a father corrects a child in whom he delights.*
PROVERBS 3:11–12 NLT

Have you ever felt adored? Been esteemed and regarded with
the utmost love, respect, and honor?

During pregnancy, you might feel like you're walking through
a season of discipline, not adoration. You're being stretched
physically. But you might also feel like you're being pushed and
pulled hormonally, emotionally, and so on. You might wonder
where God is in all of this. You might question whether you'll ever
get your body back or feel like your old self again. How could
God really adore you in these moments of angst and frustration?

Remember this: God disciplines those He loves and adores.
So take heart in knowing that you are loved immensely! You
might feel like pregnancy is discipline and hard work. In a way
it is. Why? Because it's training you to depend more on God
and to love another in ways that you're unable to on your
own. Only a few more weeks to go and you will get to meet
this little person!

---

*Father, help me to keep my eyes fixed on You.
Thank You for using this pregnancy to stretch
my faith. Show me how to adore You.*

Freely Offered

Then the people rejoiced because these had given willingly, for with a whole and blameless heart they had offered freely to the Lord. King David also rejoiced greatly. Therefore David blessed the Lord before all the assembly and said, Be praised, adored, and thanked, O Lord, the God of Israel our (forefather), forever and ever.

1 CHRONICLES 29:9–10 AMPC

"Ladies, have you ever taken the time to just praise God?" the speaker asked the moms' group. "I mean really taken the time to praise God. I'm talking like one hour of your day."

There was a moment of silence.

"Last year when I was in my third trimester with my son, I had to go on bed rest. For any of you in this room who have been on bed rest or had a very uncomfortable last trimester of pregnancy, you know you have an ample amount of time to sit around. The hardest part is you don't want to sit because there's so much to do. You lose control and feel unproductive. After several days of feeling frustrated, my husband encouraged me to use this as a time to praise God. It wasn't what I wanted to do. In fact, it's always easier for me to praise God when I'm feeling good or life is going well. So this was a challenge for me."

Father, as I start to feel uncomfortable during this pregnancy, help me to turn my pain into praise.

Enthusiastic Upholders

And upon hearing it, they adored and exalted and
praised and thanked God. And they said to (Paul),
You see, brother, how many thousands of believers
there are among the Jews, and all of them are
enthusiastic upholders of the (Mosaic) Law.
ACTS 21:20 AMPC

The speaker at the moms' group continued to share about how she praised God during bed rest.

"Ladies, it wasn't easy. But after the first forty-eight hours I had read a significant amount of the Bible and prayed for family members and friends I hadn't prayed for in a really long time. I prayed for our son: his name, his delivery, his life. While I didn't get a lot done around the house, I did get a lot done spiritually!"

The speaker talked about how she learned what it meant to truly adore God. "Before this pregnancy I thought I knew what it meant to adore God. Now I understand what it means to be an enthusiastic upholder. Someone who praises God in all things, through all things. So here's my challenge for you, ladies: How can you praise God no matter what? Who have you meant to pray for, but haven't? What circumstances or breakthroughs are you waiting on? This is a time when God might want to birth something new in you, in order to increase your faith."

Father, help me to praise You throughout this
pregnancy, but don't let it stop there. Help
me to praise You long after this baby is born.

Admiration Offering

Yours, LORD, is the greatness and the power and the glory and the majesty and the splendor, for everything in heaven and earth is yours. Yours, LORD, is the kingdom; you are exalted as head over all.
1 CHRONICLES 29:11 NIV

As the speaker continued to share with the moms, one of the group's leaders handed out white sheets of paper and some pens.

"Ladies, the sheet of paper you're getting is an assignment I have for you. We're going to take the next ten minutes to write down our praises to God. No matter where you're at, whether today has already been a challenging day or perhaps a good one, I want you to find something to praise God for. Try to write down at least five things if not more. When we're done, we're going to let them be an admiration offering to God. I'll explain more in a little bit."

Today, find a sheet of paper or a journal. Take at least ten minutes to write down at least five things that you want to praise God for. Then read each one out loud and consider it an admiration offering to God. Watch how it will change your perspective.

Father, I want my life to be filled with admiration offerings to You. I desire for this pregnancy to be an admiration offering to You! Show me how to praise You even when I find it hard to remember to, or when I don't feel like it.

On the Lookout

For I declare to you, you will not see Me again until
you say, Blessed (magnified in worship, adored,
and exalted) is He Who comes in the name of the Lord!
MATTHEW 23:39 AMPC

After the ten minutes was up, the moms shared with each other the praises they'd written down. For about half an hour the women shared some of the joys and sorrows they had recently experienced. Several of the moms were currently pregnant, dealing with various physical and spiritual challenges leading up to conception and delivery. In all of it these moms saw God's mighty hand of favor over them, their families, and their babies. For that, they praised God.

As the speaker closed she prayed for the moms. "Father God, You are awesome! We thank You for what You have done in the lives of each and every one of these moms. We don't deserve Your goodness, but we thank You for it. We adore You, Jesus! For all of us moms in this room—from those who are pregnant and expecting, to those who are about to become empty-nesters— we desire to be enthusiastic upholders of Your Word. Help us to be on the lookout for You! In Jesus' name. Amen."

Father, thank You for the little blessings You've provided me
with throughout this pregnancy. From the kicks, to the pokes
and prods, to the swelling and stretch marks, I praise You!

The Giver

And the Lord *spoke to Moses, saying, "Speak to all the
congregation of the children of Israel, and say to them:
'You shall be holy, for I the* Lord *your God am holy.
'Every one of you shall revere his mother and his father,
and keep My Sabbaths: I am the* Lord *your God.' "*
Leviticus 19:1–3 nkjv

With ten weeks left of your pregnancy, now is a great mile
marker in the mommy-to-be calling. It's time to reflect on this
journey and praise God for all that He has done.

Set aside some time for personal reflection. Be as creative
as you'd like, but write down at least five things you are thankful for in this mommy-to-be season. Here are some examples:

- God, I praise You for allowing me to conceive this child.

- God, I praise You for the times when I've been able to
  get some good sleep.

- God, I praise You for the medical team I've been working with.

- God, I praise You for the first time I heard this baby's
  heartbeat.

- God, I praise You for the first time I saw this baby through
  an ultrasound.

- God, I praise You for the times I've had good doctor
  appointments and good test results.

---

*Father, there really is so much to be thankful for! I adore You,
Jesus, for all of the blessings You have bestowed upon me.*

WEEK 30

Anointed

Your third trimester is well
under way. With this trimester
may come fatigue, clumsiness,
and the infamous nesting instinct.

Calming the Calamity

The Spirit of the Lord (is) upon Me, because He has anointed Me (the Anointed One, the Messiah) to preach the good news (the Gospel) to the poor; He has sent Me to announce release to the captives and recovery of sight to the blind, to send forth as delivered those who are oppressed (who are downtrodden, bruised, crushed, and broken down by calamity).
LUKE 4:18 AMPC

Diana was thirty weeks pregnant with her second child when she stumbled her way into the kitchen. Her feet weren't playing tricks on her because of her growing waistline. Her legs nearly went out from underneath her because her three-year-old son had been playing trucks in the kitchen. He left several of his toys on the floor en route to the family room.

Thankfully, Diana was able to reach for the kitchen counter and brace herself. As she stood up, she could feel her blood pressure rising. She was already feeling the effects of the nesting instinct welling up within her. She leaned over toward the refrigerator and caught a glimpse of a Bible verse held by a magnet. Diana read it, took a few deep breaths, and thanked God for helping her not to fall and raise her voice at her son.

Father, there's so much to do before this baby arrives. I have so much on my mind too. Please calm the calamity within me with Your words and Your presence.

Saving Strength

The LORD is my strength and my shield; my heart trusted in him, and I am helped: therefore my heart greatly rejoiceth; and with my song will I praise him. The LORD is their strength, and he is the saving strength of his anointed.
PSALM 28:7–8 KJV

Psalm 28:7–8 was the scripture that Diana had on her refrigerator. It was the passage that stared straight at her while she braced herself from falling over her son's toys scattered on the kitchen floor. She clung to this scripture as she prayed for this pregnancy. She and her husband had a hard time conceiving their second baby, and this verse gave Diana hope.

This second pregnancy seemed fraught with calamity. Just when one aspect of the pregnancy would settle down, like morning sickness or fatigue, another concern would creep up. Diana clung to the belief that no matter how tumultuous this pregnancy became, God had promised her a second child. She believed she was anointed for the mommy-to-be task despite her circumstances.

As you brace yourself for these last ten weeks or so of pregnancy, reflect on how the Lord has been your strength. Remember that He anointed you to be a mommy-to-be and He will continue to remain faithful to you through it all.

Father, thank You for letting me be a mommy-to-be. This pregnancy has gone so fast. I praise You for being my strength throughout all of it.

Anointed Ones

So he said, "These are the two anointed ones,
who stand beside the Lord of the whole earth."
ZECHARIAH 4:14 NKJV

As a mommy-to-be, you have been anointed for a life-giving and life-changing responsibility. Those who are anointed are consecrated or dedicated to the service of God. It's a calling that will bring you great rewards in this life and in eternity with Jesus.

You might not feel like you have what it takes to fulfill the daily demands. That's okay, because you don't need to. All you need is Jesus. When you are in those moments of doubt and questioning, as you might already be at thirty weeks pregnant, just call out His name. His name is above all names. Jesus was anointed too.

So take some time today to walk through your own anointing process. First, place your hands on your belly. Then, as you feel your baby kick, pray for them. Pray for yourself too: for strength, wisdom, mercy, and grace as you interact with the baby. Invite the Holy Spirit to fill your body, especially your womb, and just talk to God. Remember: He loves you, and He wants to hear from you!

Father, thank You that I always have access to You.
When I'm by myself parenting this baby, I want
to parent with You. Please lead me, guide me,
and direct me in everything I say and do.

Sanctified

Laura was excited. She had received a text message from her friend Janelle saying that she was looking forward to seeing Laura at her baby shower. At thirty weeks pregnant, Laura was looking forward to seeing many of her friends too.

Laura lived in a different state than where she grew up, but through work and church ministry, she was able to connect with many other women, some of whom were also pregnant and due around the same time as she was. Laura felt like she and her husband had a good support system.

Laura knew that some of her friends were organizing a baby shower. She loved creating the baby registry and picking out specific items. Yet with each item she added to the registry, she started to feel overwhelmed. Laura wondered how to use some of the different baby gadgets and gizmos. The more she studied some of the items, the more doubt drifted into her mind.

Father, I come to Your altar asking for Your wisdom and guidance. God, as I register for my shower or unpack old baby stuff to use once again, please bless each item that I use. Please give me wisdom for how to use everything.

Created for Good

You were anointed as a guardian cherub, for so I ordained you. You were on the holy mount of God; you walked among the fiery stones. You were blameless in your ways from the day you were created till wickedness was found in you.
EZEKIEL 28:14–15 NIV

Ezekiel was created for a purpose. He was anointed by God to go into a prophetic ministry. A ministry that would help steer people back to God. An anointed ministry that would help people turn from their wicked ways, be humble, and ask God for forgiveness.

You were created for a purpose too. God has anointed you for a task. Currently, you are a mommy-to-be. God is using your body to create a new life that will also have a purpose, a calling that is anointed by God. Right now, as you prepare to welcome this baby into the world, you can be praying for all of the plans and good works God has in store for this baby boy or girl. Just think, one day your baby might be a mouthpiece to the nations—an instrument used by God for His divine glory!

Lord, thank You for creating me. Thank You for knitting me together inside my mother's womb. Thank You for giving me life and breath. Help me to continue to live out this mommy-to-be calling. Lead me to do good works because of what You have done in and through me, so that others can see Your love and grace.

One-of-a-Kind

"He said, 'Watch closely. Notice that all the goats
in the flock that are mating are streaked, speckled,
and mottled. I know what Laban's been doing to you.
I'm the God of Bethel where you consecrated a pillar
and made a vow to me. Now be on your way, get out
of this place, go home to your birthplace.' "
GENESIS 31:12–13 MSG

As you prepare for the birth of your baby, think about where you were born. Do you know which hospital it was? Or were you born in a different setting? What city and state were you born in? All of these questions are meaningful for you to reflect on and consider as you prepare for the delivery of your own child. Why? Because the answers tell a story. A story about who you are. Where you were born and grew up helped shape you into the person you are today.

The same is true for your baby. Take some time today to consider how you would like to remember this information and share it when your baby is old enough to understand. Consider creating a baby book or a journal to write down this one-of-a-kind information. Pray about how you'd like to celebrate this information as a part of their story.

Father, as a child of God, I'm grateful for all of the unique
things about me. Thank You for making me special and
different. Show me how to celebrate my baby's unique story.

Sentimentally Sacred

"Aaron's sacred garments must be preserved for his descendants who succeed him, and they will wear them when they are anointed and ordained. The descendant who succeeds him as high priest will wear these clothes for seven days as he ministers in the Tabernacle and the Holy Place."
EXODUS 29:29–30 NLT

In the book of Exodus, Aaron was a high priest—and he was the older brother of Moses. His garments were considered sacred; important enough that the clothes were meant to be passed on to his descendants.

It might still be ten or so weeks away, but have you thought about what you'd like to bring your baby home in? Obviously, you'll have a car seat for your kiddo. And if you know the gender of your baby bump, then that might make this clothing decision a little easier.

Either way, the first outfit they wear home is something to consider. If there's one piece of clothing you may want to be sentimental about, it's the first outfit you dress your baby in when you bring them home. It's one that you will probably take a few photos of them in. It's a piece of clothing that you might set apart for them to see and keep when they get older.

Father, please give me wisdom in remembering my baby's birth. Show me what to keep and hold on to as a way to celebrate and cherish my baby and their birthday.

WEEK 31

♡

Clothed

As you prepare for the baby's arrival, you might be blessed with baby clothing from a baby shower or hand-me-downs.

Surprise!

In a desert land he found him, in a barren and howling waste. He shielded him and cared for him; he guarded him as the apple of his eye, like an eagle that stirs up its nest and hovers over its young, that spreads its wings to catch them and carries them aloft.
DEUTERONOMY 32:10–11 NIV

Crystal was so excited she could hardly wait! She and some of her friends from the moms' group were getting ready to throw a big surprise baby shower for their friend Gabby. Gabby was thirty-one weeks pregnant. She and her husband had only been in town for about a year. They had no family close by, and this was their first baby. Because Gabby's childhood and college friends lived all over the world, the moms' group felt compelled to bless her.

Crystal was also a mommy-to-be, about the same number of weeks along as Gabby. But this was Crystal's third pregnancy. She felt like she got to be not only a friend to Gabby, but a mentor. For Crystal, it was fun to remember what it was like to be pregnant for the first time. She was grateful to be part of blessing Gabby's new addition.

Father, I'm grateful that in this mommy-to-be stage of life You've blessed me with many other moms who understand what it's like to walk through this calling. Continue to show me how I can be a friend and mentor to other new moms.

Enough Clothes

"That is why I tell you not to worry about everyday life—whether you have enough food and drink, or enough clothes to wear. Isn't life more than food, and your body more than clothing? Look at the birds. They don't plant or harvest or store food in barns, for your heavenly Father feeds them. And aren't you far more valuable to him than they are? Can all your worries add a single moment to your life?"
MATTHEW 6:25–27 NLT

Gwen couldn't believe it. Some of the women in her moms' group at church decided to give all of their hand-me-down baby clothes to her. Gwen was thirty-one weeks pregnant with her first baby, and many of the moms were in the process of organizing their baby stuff.

Gwen left the moms' meeting with four 13-gallon bags full of clothes. As she placed each bag in the trunk of her sedan, she began to cry. She was so thankful. She hadn't had a baby shower yet, but receiving these clothes calmed a lot of her anxiety.

Gwen's husband had recently lost his job and was in the process of looking for a new one. She pleaded with God to provide for their needs, and the bags of clothes for her baby were a reminder that He knew what their family needed most.

Father, thank You for providing for all of my needs. When I feel anxious about how I'm going to pay for things, help me to remember that You will provide.

What to Wear

"So why do you worry about clothing? Consider the lilies of the field, how they grow: they neither toil nor spin; and yet I say to you that even Solomon in all his glory was not arrayed like one of these. Now if God so clothes the grass of the field, which today is, and tomorrow is thrown into the oven, will He not much more clothe you, O you of little faith?"
MATTHEW 6:28–30 NKJV

Jesus spoke about not worrying. Why? Because He doesn't want you to worry. Sounds easier said than done, right?

As a mommy-to-be, you probably have had your fair share of things to worry about. During the first trimester, it was dealing with fatigue or weird food cravings.

Then came the second trimester. While you might have started to feel like your energy was coming back, your baby bump became more noticeable.

Now the third trimester can leave you scrambling for some comfort and rest as you worry about whether you'll have enough stamina to make it a few more weeks.

While Jesus was using clothing as a metaphor for not worrying, he meant not to worry about anything. He knows exactly what you need now and in the future. If you really are wondering if this is true, just ask Him.

Father, I'm going to make a choice today not to worry so much about all of the details of this pregnancy. I'm going to choose to focus those thoughts on You!

Seams

Focus not on the daunting details, but hone in on the One who
makes all the seams come together: Jesus.

As you read today's devotional, do you feel distracted or
focused? It's time to take a little inventory on how you are doing. Take a few deep breaths and ask God to intervene. Share
with Him your cares about the remainder of this pregnancy.
Here's a place to start:

- Jesus, I'm worried about how much weight I've gained.

- Jesus, I'm worried today about this baby. Keep my baby
  safe. What will my delivery be like?

- Jesus, I'm tired. When will I be able to sleep well again?

- Jesus, I'm worried about all of the finances and details
  required to raise this baby and give them what they need.

- Jesus, I'm concerned that breastfeeding will be
  uncomfortable.

- Jesus, I'm concerned I won't have enough help before
  and after the baby arrives.

*Father, I have a lot I'm concerned about. Keep my eyes
fixed on You, the One who sews everything together.*

The Stark Reality

Adam named his wife Eve, because she would become the mother of all the living. The Lᴏʀᴅ God made garments of skin for Adam and his wife and clothed them.
Gᴇɴᴇsɪs 3:20–21 ɴɪᴠ

It's a humbling reality to consider that ever since the beginning of creation, all this world has needed is God. Ever since the creation of Adam, all people have needed is God. It was God who provided Eve. It was God who provided skin and clothing for them. Everything was provided for because God was their earthly and heavenly Father.

As a mommy-to-be, the same holds true for you. Everything you have ever needed, and will need, comes from your eternal Father. You might think you need people, like your parents, your siblings, your grandparents, your spouse, your aunt or uncle, to help you out. But the stark reality is that all you need is God. He is the giver of everything you need. He is the provider of all the help you will ever need. He is the ultimate source, who showers you with blessings and provision.

Father, thank You for providing for me and this baby. It's humbling as a mommy-to-be, to realize that all my baby really needs is You. Yes, they will have needs as they come into this world and grow up. But they actually need You more than they need me. So in all that I do, please help me point them to You and Your grace.

Treat Yourself

Denise and her husband moved to a new town shortly before becoming pregnant with their first child. They were about five hundred miles away from any family members or close friends. Starting over wasn't easy for them—they'd lived in the same state for much of their life.

Denise did the best she could to get to know people, including other women at the moms' group she attended through church.

When she was thirty-one weeks pregnant, the moms' group threw her a baby shower. She had some indication that the group was going to bless her, because a couple of the leaders had asked if she would be coming to the meeting, and where she'd registered for baby items.

While the baby shower was a huge blessing, Denise's favorite gift of all was a gift card for her to get a manicure and pedicure. With it was a note that read: *Please use this to treat yourself.* The moms' love toward Denise left an impression upon her to pray about how she could bless others she barely even knew.

Father, as a mommy-to-be, please give me the wisdom and courage to love and bless others I barely even know.

Clothed in Christ

Dear friends, do you think you'll get anywhere in this if
you learn all the right words but never do anything?
Does merely talking about faith indicate that a person really
has it? For instance, you come upon an old friend dressed
in rags and half-starved and say, "Good morning, friend!
Be clothed in Christ! Be filled with the Holy Spirit!" and walk
off without providing so much as a coat or a cup of soup—
where does that get you? Isn't it obvious that God-talk
without God-acts is outrageous nonsense?
JAMES 2:14–17 MSG

James stressed the importance of faith in action. Actions aren't what save a person, but they are an extension and expression of the faith you possess.

As a mommy-to-be, you're taking a big step of faith to welcome a baby into this world. You are relying on God every step of the way for the comfort, care, and provision of this child. Having a baby changes your whole life. It changes your perspective and outlook on who God is for you: your heavenly Father.

So be clothed in Christ today. As you put on your maternity wear, thank God for each garment. If someone gave it to you or helped you buy it, pray for that person too.

Father, every step of the way in this pregnancy,
help me to pray for each person who has been
a part of this season and calling with me.

WEEK 32

Honored

As you and your baby continue to grow, some new symptoms might emerge, such as fatigue or heartburn.

Dedicated to God

*Eight days later, when the baby was circumcised,
he was named Jesus, the name given him by the
angel even before he was conceived. Then it was
time for their purification offering, as required by the
law of Moses after the birth of a child; so his parents
took him to Jerusalem to present him to the Lord.*
LUKE 2:21–22 NLT

Mary and Joseph were doing what was required of them as
parents. According to the Law of Moses, they took their son to
be circumcised and gave Him the name they were led to name
Him—Jesus. After that, they went to Jerusalem to present Jesus
to the Lord. In essence, Mary and Joseph were dedicating their
son, God's one and only Son, back to God. In doing all of these
things, Mary and Joseph honored God and Jesus. In return, God
looked favorably upon them, for they were set apart.

As a mommy-to-be, you might not feel it or see it yet, but
you're walking through the good old days. This is because you
need God's help all the time, every time, 24-7. You are completely dependent on God right now. Once the baby arrives,
you are that much more dependent on God. So as Mary and
Joseph remained dedicated to the Old Testament law, remain
dedicated to leaning into God's grace and mercy.

*Father, I dedicate this pregnancy and this child to You!
I desire for 1 Corinthians 6:19–20 to be my prayer to You!*

258

Before the Lord

*When her husband Elkanah went up with all his family
to offer the annual sacrifice to the Lord and to fulfill his
vow, Hannah did not go. She said to her husband, "After
the boy is weaned, I will take him and present him
before the Lord, and he will live there always."*
1 Samuel 1:21–22 niv

Hannah presented her son to the Lord after he was weaned.
Hannah had prayed fervently for this precious gift of life. So
when she became pregnant, she knew this special blessing was
from the Lord. God heard her prayers. Rightfully so, Hannah
felt that it was right to present Samuel to God, showing honor
and reverence to God for His grace on her womb.

As you read this devotional, you might feel your baby
moving around inside of your womb. For a few minutes, take
some time to reflect on how far God has brought you through
this pregnancy. Think back on the journey you walked through
in order to conceive. Reflect on the first trimester, the second,
and now the third. Honor God with your words and praise Him
for all that He has done. Consider how you might continue to
go before the Lord, honoring Him for what He has done.

*Father, You are so worthy of my praise! From the very
depths of my soul I thank You for carrying me through
this mommy-to-be calling and season of life.*

Crowned

Emily placed her hand on her round, firm belly. At thirty-two weeks pregnant, she could feel a Braxton Hicks contraction. She sat down in a chair nestled between the kitchen and her daughter's play nook. Emily sat and watched as her daughter pretended to be a princess. Her three-year-old wore a tiara, a play dress, and some jewelry.

As Emily leaned back into the chair, she could feel her pregnant body sink in. She tried her best to take a few deep breaths—a commodity that was hard to come by these days. But as she felt each breath go in and out, she remembered her grandfather. He passed away before her daughter was born. Her papa would play tea with her, and he called her his princess.

As Emily got older, her grandfather shared more of his faith with her. It was in that moment that Emily committed to pray for the baby inside of her womb. She and her husband didn't know the gender yet. If it was a boy, she wanted to somehow honor her grandfather's legacy by giving the baby his name.

Father, help me to pass on my faith to my baby. Show me how I can honor You through this child, and show me how I can bless my family members with this gift of life.

Good Gifts

*"If you then, being evil, know how to give good gifts to
your children, how much more will your Father who is in
heaven give good things to those who ask Him!"*
MATTHEW 7:11 NKJV

What did Jesus mean when He called His listeners evil? He
wasn't trying to condemn them. Instead the use of the word
evil is meant to be a reminder that He came to save sinners:
imperfect people who make imperfect choices in life. It's freeing
to recognize imperfections because that means God is on the
throne in your mommy-to-be life!

Imperfections bring great qualities though. They bring
humility and the need to lean on God's grace and mercy
on a daily basis. They lead you to ask Jesus for help, wisdom,
discernment, and other good gifts.

So as you gear up to be showered with good gifts from
friends and family for your baby, remember that you also get
to partake in the showering of good gifts from your heavenly
Father. He wants to lavish you with everything you need to
have this baby. All you need to do is ask!

---

*Oh Lord, I need You! Help me to remember the
reality of my sin. My ugly sin that nailed You to the
cross. Thank You for allowing me to recognize my
imperfections and to experience Your abundant
grace and mercy in this mommy-to-be season of life.*

A Peculiar Treasure

Now therefore, if ye will obey my voice indeed, and keep my covenant, then ye shall be a peculiar treasure unto me above all people: for all the earth is mine: and ye shall be unto me a kingdom of priests, and an holy nation. These are the words which thou shalt speak unto the children of Israel.

EXODUS 19:5–6 KJV

In the book of Exodus, Moses spoke to the Israelites about the importance of obeying God. If they obeyed God, they would be considered a peculiar treasure—a treasured possession. Their obedience honored God, and in return He would also honor them as a special nation. A nation that would be blessed and looked favorably upon.

Being a mommy-to-be is a great opportunity to glorify, or honor, God through your body. Did you know that God wants to honor you too? As you continue to live in obedience to God, His grace and mercy will continue to abound in your life. You will be aware of His presence and blessings.

Reflect on your reverence for God. Consider what it must have been like for the Israelites to receive this promise from God. Accept that this is a promise God wants to fulfill through you too.

Father, give me the strength to remain faithfully obedient to You. I love You, Lord. As a mommy-to-be I desire to be Your treasured possession.

Recognized

*I in them and You in Me, in order that they may
become one and perfectly united, that the world may
know and (definitely) recognize that You sent Me and that
You have loved them (even) as You have loved Me.*
JOHN 17:23 AMPC

Layla was speechless. She wasn't expecting to see so many
familiar faces at her baby shower. Her sister-in-law had orga-
nized the event. Layla had hoped and prayed to see certain
women attend. Instead she was blessed by over thirty women,
all of them friends in different seasons of life. Some of them
were expecting their first baby, while others were expecting
their second or third. And then there were women who had
teenagers or who were about to be empty-nesters.

"Layla, you might not feel it right now, but cherish this moment. Cherish the fact that God is using your body to create
the miracle of life!" one of her friends encouraged her.

"It's an honor and a privilege to be a mom, Layla," another
friend told her.

"I'm grateful to have you as a friend and to be walking
through this journey with you," another friend added.

Layla felt very supported by the simple act of women
showing up to shower her and the baby.

---

*Father, thank You for providing me with women
who have supported and encouraged me as a
mommy-to-be. I'm so grateful for how You have
blessed my life through their love for me.*

Dependable Dependence

"Here's what I'm saying: Ask and you'll get; seek and you'll find; knock and the door will open. Don't bargain with God. Be direct. Ask for what you need. This is not a cat-and-mouse, hide-and-seek game we're in. If your little boy asks for a serving of fish, do you scare him with a live snake on his plate? If your little girl asks for an egg, do you trick her with a spider? As bad as you are, you wouldn't think of such a thing—you're at least decent to your own children. And don't you think the Father who conceived you in love will give the Holy Spirit when you ask him?"

LUKE 11:9–13 MSG

Being a mommy-to-be calls you to step into an area of life where you might feel physically and emotionally weak. It places you in a prominent position to fully depend on God's grace and mercy, which are what your true identity in Jesus Christ is rooted in.

Did you know that when you depend fully on God you are honoring or respecting His position as Lord? You are! It's the most dependable dependence you can count on!

Father, thank You that when I'm weak I'm also strong! When I'm weak in myself, I get to tap into Your strength through the power of the Holy Spirit. May Your Spirit empower me to glorify You. Thank You that I get to honor You in this way!

WEEK 33

Awakened

You might start to feel like you're waddling more than walking. As for sleeping, you might have a hard time getting comfortable when you're waking up several times at night.

Up at Night

Good friend, take to heart what I'm telling you; collect my counsels and guard them with your life. Tune your ears to the world of Wisdom; set your heart on a life of Understanding. That's right—if you make Insight your priority, and won't take no for an answer, searching for it like a prospector panning for gold, like an adventurer on a treasure hunt, believe me, before you know it Fear-of-God will be yours; you'll have come upon the Knowledge of God.
PROVERBS 2:1–5 MSG

Solomon, the writer of the book of Proverbs, gave some great advice. He encouraged his readers to heed wisdom, because with it comes many benefits. Benefits in this world and in eternity.

As a mommy-to-be, you hear a lot of great advice regarding pregnancy. A lot of it is very helpful. Yet sometimes, especially if this is your first pregnancy, you might feel a bit overwhelmed by what you can and can't eat, what you need to buy, what you need to read, and the list goes on and on. It's enough to keep you awake at night!

Take some time to pray about what is the best advice you need. Ask God to guide and direct your thoughts, your purchases, and your ability to receive wise counsel.

Father, there's so much good advice out there. Help me to make sense of it all. Help me to process what I need right away and what I can put on reserve for later.

A Fresh Heart

So, friends, take a firm stand, feet on the ground and head
high. Keep a tight grip on what you were taught, whether
in personal conversation or by our letter. May Jesus himself
and God our Father, who reached out in love and surprised
you with gifts of unending help and confidence, put a fresh
heart in you, invigorate your work, enliven your speech.
2 THESSALONIANS 2:16–17 MSG

The apostle Paul encouraged the Thessalonian believers to hold on tightly to their faith. As they held tightly to their beliefs, God would refresh and revive their spirits.

Another word for awakened is *revived*. Think back on this pregnancy and consider a time when you felt revived, or when God put a fresh spirit within you. Maybe it was during your second trimester when you had more energy or got a good night's sleep. Perhaps it was recently when you got to attend your baby shower. Or maybe it was seeing ultrasound pictures or hearing your baby's heartbeat.

Whatever it may be, hold tightly to God in these moments. God is the Creator of life and the giver of good things. Hold tightly to His love and goodness. Seek His Word. Follow His counsel, and watch as your spirit is awakened to God's goodness.

Father, continue to revive my spirit as I continue this
pregnancy journey. When I feel tired and weary,
lift me up. Help me to stay focused on You and
not my circumstances or feelings.

Awaken Me

Remember your promise to me; it is my only hope.
Your promise revives me; it comforts me in all my
troubles. The proud hold me in utter contempt,
but I do not turn away from your instructions.
PSALM 119:49–51 NLT

Sally came to moms' group in tears. She felt defeated, rejected, and frustrated. She shared that a family member thought she was gaining too much weight. At thirty-three weeks pregnant, she had gained thirty-five pounds.

"Oh Sally!" one of the moms consoled her, "You look beautiful! Please don't worry about how much weight you've gained."

Another mom, who had four kids, shared her story.

"Sally, with each pregnancy I gained fifty pounds. I lost all of it within a year after having each of my kids. I remember feeling the same way you do during my first and second pregnancies. But then I realized that this is just how God made my body. With the third and fourth I accepted it. It's okay."

Hearing the other moms share their stories, and some of the scripture verses they clung to during the most difficult times of their pregnancies, revived Sally. It gave her the encouragement she needed to read more about what God says about her.

Father, during this pregnancy there are times when
I'm tempted not to see myself the way that You do.
In those moments, awaken my spirit so that I may fix
my mind on what You have to say about me.

Awaken the Dawn

My heart is steadfast, O God, my heart is steadfast; I will sing
and give praise. Awake, my glory! Awake, lute and harp!
I will awaken the dawn. I will praise You, O Lord, among
the peoples; I will sing to You among the nations.
PSALM 57:7–9 NKJV

David praised God by expressing his complete and total dependence on Him. David didn't hold back though. He shared his concerns with God and ended with praise.

Here you are at thirty-three weeks pregnant. You're almost done! At this point you might have more concerns than praises to share with God. So take some time today to do the following:

- Share with God how you feel. Let Him know your deep worries, cares, and concerns.

- As you share each mommy-to-be concern, thank Him for letting you come to Him with vulnerability. Ask God to fill you with a fresh presence of the Holy Spirit.

- When you feel like you're done sharing your concerns with God, praise Him. Ask Him to help you remember times when He was faithful. Praise God for those moments. Ask Him to fill you with hope and an assurance that He's with you.

Father, when I come to You with my cares and
concerns—even though the situation might not change—
I do become refreshed. I'm awakened to the reality of
who You are during this mommy-to-be season of life.

Sunrise

My heart, O God, is steadfast; I will sing and make music with
all my soul. Awake, harp and lyre! I will awaken the dawn.
I will praise you, LORD, among the nations; I will sing of you
among the peoples. For great is your love, higher than the
heavens; your faithfulness reaches to the skies. Be exalted, O
God, above the heavens; let your glory be over all the earth.
PSALM 108:1–5 NIV

Desiree woke up several times during the middle of the night.
With seven weeks left in her pregnancy, she had to make a
lot more visits to the bathroom. Her middle-of-the-night trips
created quite a disturbance in her sleep schedule. She felt
exhausted, and it was hard for her to get comfortable.

Desiree wasn't sure what else to do, so she reached for
her phone and read through her Bible reading plan. She read
Psalm 108 and realized it had been a long time since she'd
seen a sunrise. She decided to get up and go downstairs into
the kitchen where she could see the sun come up. As it did she
could feel the baby move and kick. Desiree rubbed her belly
and praised God for waking her up to experience His beauty.

Father, I don't like feeling uncomfortable, having to go
to the bathroom a lot, or having a hard time sleeping.
I trust that there is a blessing in these hardships though.
Please help me to have the eyes to see Your goodness.

Get Up!

*And suddenly an angel of the Lord appeared
(standing beside him), and a light shone in the
place where he was. And the angel gently smote
Peter on the side and awakened him, saying,
Get up quickly! And the chains fell off his hands.*

ACTS 12:7 AMPC

Sandra was literally beside herself. So much so that she couldn't get up. She managed to get down on the floor to put her shoes on, but then she couldn't get herself back up. She tried with all of her might, and due to the stress of it all she started having some Braxton Hicks contractions.

"Jesse, I need your help, please," she asked her husband.

Jesse walked into the mudroom to see his wife sitting on the floor. He smiled and reached out both of his hands to help pull her up. As she stood up and got her footing, Jesse embraced her with a big hug.

"I love you, Sandra," he said and gave her a big kiss on the forehead. "And I love you too, baby, even with all you're doing to make Mommy uncomfortable," he said with his hands on her baby bump.

"Thank you," Sandra said with some tears in her eyes. "Thank you for loving me and helping me even in the state I'm in."

---

*Father, thank You for lifting my spirit, removing my
chains, and pardoning my sins so that I can be
free to be the mommy-to-be that I am.*

A Vision

And the angel that talked with me came again,
and waked me, as a man that is wakened out of his sleep.
ZECHARIAH 4:1 KJV

Renee woke up during the middle of the night. At thirty-three weeks pregnant she had been dealing with trips to the bathroom, discomfort, and leg cramps. But this time she woke up because of a dream she'd had. In the dream, she dreamed that she was giving birth to her baby. The dream startled her, and she woke up wondering if it was true or not.

Startled by the vision, Renee put both of her hands on her belly. A sense of peace came over her as she realized she was okay, and so was her baby. Her bump was still intact. She got up from her bed and walked into the bathroom. It was there she prayed out loud for her and the baby. She prayed for God's peace over her mind too.

As she waddled her way back to bed, her husband woke up. Wondering if everything was okay, he prayed for her too. The two snuggled themselves back to sleep, and Renee slept well for the rest of the night.

Father, pregnancy is causing my body to do some weird things. All of this stuff that keeps waking me up at night, I ask that You would have power, authority, and control over it. Please help me to get a good night's sleep so I can wake up feeling refreshed.

WEEK 34

♡

Imagined

As you and your baby continue
to grow, dizziness and fatigue
may be slowing you down.

God's Great Legacy

Then God said, "Let us make human beings in our image, to be like us. They will reign over the fish in the sea, the birds in the sky, the livestock, all the wild animals on the earth, and the small animals that scurry along the ground." So God created human beings in his own image. In the image of God he created them; male and female he created them. Then God blessed them and said, "Be fruitful and multiply. Fill the earth and govern it. Reign over the fish in the sea, the birds in the sky, and all the animals that scurry along the ground."
GENESIS 1:26–28 NLT

God created you for a purpose. His plan was that man and woman, created in His image, would bring Him glory.

Through Adam and Eve, sin entered the scene, which gave way to an imperfect, fallen world. A world that bore His image, mercy, love, and grace. But also a world tainted by sin that gave way to consequences. A world that needed a Savior to forgive and cleanse us from unrighteousness.

As a mommy-to-be, you're continuing God's great legacy: to be fruitful and multiply. To fill the whole earth with image bearers—His children. As you do, you're a blessing to God and to others just as He imagined.

Father, may I continue to walk this mommy-to-be journey with You. May I continue to pass on the great legacy that You imagined found in Genesis 1:26–2:4.

Imagine That!

From one man he made all the nations, that they should inhabit the whole earth; and he marked out their appointed times in history and the boundaries of their lands. God did this so that they would seek him and perhaps reach out for him and find him, though he is not far from any one of us.

ACTS 17:26–27 NIV

Lauren was feeling frazzled. At thirty-four weeks pregnant, she could feel the anxiety welling up inside of her. It seemed like there was a lot to do before the baby came. She was tired, worn out, achy, and emotional.

Lauren decided she needed to get in to see her counselor. As soon as she stepped foot into her counselor's office, all of her emotions poured out of her eyes. Lauren was crying so hard she could feel a few Braxton Hicks contractions.

A few minutes into her counseling session, Lauren felt a little better. She was able to breathe a bit deeper (or as deeply as she could these days). She saw a glimpse of hope as her counselor quoted scripture and reminded her that God was near. And He was.

Father, You're right here with me! Even as I read this devotion and prayer, You're right next to me. When I have moments of deep despair, help me to close my eyes, take a few deep breaths, meditate on Your Word, and imagine that You're standing right next to me.

His Offspring

For in Him we live and move and have our being; as even some of your (own) poets have said, For we are also His offspring. Since then we are God's offspring, we ought not to suppose that Deity (the Godhead) is like gold or silver or stone, (of the nature of) a representation by human art and imagination, or anything constructed or invented.
ACTS 17:28–29 AMPC

Gabby waddled her way into her thirty-four-week prenatal appointment. She hadn't been gaining much weight, and her medical care team recommended they do an ultrasound just to make sure everything was going okay for her and the baby.

After they wheeled in a portable ultrasound machine, she was amazed by the size of her baby. Her baby now took up double, if not more, of the space on the screen. As her doctor maneuvered the ultrasound probe around her belly, she was in awe. From the tiny hands and feet to the strong kicks.

The ultrasound showed that everything was fine with her and the baby. She learned that some women can start to plateau in their weight gain during the last few weeks of pregnancy.

Father, I'm Your offspring, and I thank You for this baby inside of me who is also Your offspring—created in a way that You imagined and designed.

Inner Framework

*My frame was not hidden from You, when I was made in
secret, and skillfully wrought in the lowest parts of the earth.
Your eyes saw my substance, being yet unformed. And in
Your book they all were written, the days fashioned for me,
when as yet there were none of them.*
PSALM 139:15–16 NKJV

David wrote a psalm to God expressing his deep humility and
reverence for God. In David's reflection, he yielded to God's
control and ability to search his heart. He acknowledged God
as the Creator and Sustainer of life.

Like many seasons in life, pregnancy can bring you to your
knees. From a physical perspective, the challenge can be
literally getting back up on your feet again and finding your
footing. But it can be equally as hard to find a sense of stability
and strength when your hormones are going crazy. Pregnancy
can bring you a deep sense of reverence and dependence
on God. Pregnancy can also help you yield to God's will and
surrender full control to Him.

All of this is great preparation for parenthood. So take it with
great joy that as He continues to mold the inner framework of
your baby, He's also molding the inner framework of your faith.

---

*Father, I've been learning so much about You during this
pregnancy. Thank You for loving me enough to care for
each delicate part of my body, as well as my baby's.
I'm grateful that You know everything about me.*

Before You Were Born

Ask questions. Find out what has been going on all these years before you were born. From the day God created man and woman on this Earth, and from the horizon in the east to the horizon in the west—as far back as you can imagine and as far away as you can imagine—has as great a thing as this ever happened? Has anyone ever heard of such a thing? Has a people ever heard, as you did, a god speaking out of the middle of the fire and lived to tell the story?
DEUTERONOMY 4:32–33 MSG

A lot happened before Jesus was born. On earth, He was prophesied about. When He came into earthly existence as King, people had their own expectations of what He should have been like. What people didn't imagine was that His gentle, humble spirit was all they needed to live a free and forgiven life on earth and for eternity.

A lot happened before you were born too. Before you were even conceived, God thought about you. He loved you with unconditional, unlimited love. Imagine that—you were first loved by God before you were conceived, before you were even born! That's amazing!

Father, Your love for me and my baby is a great mystery. Help me to get a glimpse of Your love for me so that I may offer that same love to my baby.

A Library

There are so many other things Jesus did. If they were all written down, each of them, one by one, I can't imagine a world big enough to hold such a library of books.

JOHN 21:25 MSG

Jocelyn was feeling overwhelmed. With six weeks left until her due date, she had just left her prenatal appointment. As she got into her car, she remembered that a friend from church had invited her to a moms' group.

Jocelyn decided she didn't want to be alone in her concerns, so she drove to church to meet up with the moms. Once she was there she felt like she was in the right place. It was there she found her friend Kelly and shared with her about the appointment. Jocelyn felt overwhelmed with all of the information she had to process, think through, and read about. Things like scheduling a tour of the labor and delivery ward and registering at the hospital. The list went on and on.

It was at the moms' group that Jocelyn found other women who had walked in her shoes. A library of women with faith stories to share about how God turned their most overwhelming mommy-to-be moments into opportunities to glorify Him.

Father, when I feel overwhelmed by all I still have to do in preparation for this baby, help me to lean into You and Your Word, and—if it's Your will—provide me with comfort through the experiences of other moms.

Above and Beyond

"My thoughts are nothing like your thoughts," says the LORD. *"And my ways are far beyond anything you could imagine. For just as the heavens are higher than the earth, so my ways are higher than your ways and my thoughts higher than your thoughts."*
ISAIAH 55:8–9 NLT

The prophet Isaiah invited the nation of Judah to receive the Lord's salvation. He prompted them to turn from their old way of living in order to receive the full blessings of God. Most importantly, in chapter 55, Isaiah explained just how above and beyond God was.

As a mommy-to-be, you might be feeling like you want to go back to your old way of life. A life that was filled with a good night's sleep, no aches and pains, no leg cramps, constipation, or swelling. A life filled with the ability to eat a full meal or breathe deeply. The truth is that in a few short weeks, you'll be able to go back to feeling a little bit like your old self. But there will be new blessings and challenges. You might not feel better, but if you think above and beyond like God does, you will realize you truly are a better woman because of this pregnancy.

Father, I believe that when this pregnancy is all said and done, I will be above and beyond a better child of God because of this whole experience.

WEEK 35

Affirmed

While you're starting to feel like there's barely any room left inside your womb, it will be affirming to know that you'll still be able to feel baby's kicks, pokes, and jabs.

Pregnancy Prayers

Though I walk in the midst of trouble, You will revive me; You will stretch forth Your hand against the wrath of my enemies, and Your right hand will save me. The Lord will perfect that which concerns me; Your mercy and loving-kindness, O Lord, endure forever—forsake not the works of Your own hands.

PSALM 138:7–8 AMPC

David, the writer of Psalm 138, understood what it was like to be going through troubled times. By faith he believed God would revive him. He believed by faith that God was looking out for him, taking care of him. David had firsthand experience with God's mercy and grace, and he believed God was on his side—no matter what!

As a mommy-to-be at thirty-five weeks pregnant, you might feel like you're going through some troubles of your own. There isn't a whole lot of room left in your body for the baby to maneuver around, and you might be wondering how you will ever get through the next few weeks.

Consider turning what David wrote in Psalm 138:7–8 into a pregnancy prayer. As you pray, hold out your hands with your palms facing upward and wide open. This act symbolizes that you're receiving from God all the good that He has in store for you.

Father, may the words of my mouth and the meditations of my heart be pleasing to You. Show me how to turn David's writing into a prayer that I can pray too.

A Happy Parent

Dear child, if you become wise, I'll be one happy parent. My heart will dance and sing to the tuneful truth you'll speak.
PROVERBS 23:15–16 MSG

Solomon shared with those willing to heed instruction about the importance of living a life in reverence and obedience to God. In Proverbs 23:15–16, Solomon speaks about how God will be a happy Father. Your heavenly Father already loves you regardless of the wise or unwise choices you make. But to really make Him proud is to become wise.

As a mommy-to-be, how do you become wise? There's already so much to do. There's already so much everybody else might be sharing with you or telling you that you need to do, to buy, to wear. But one of the most important things you can do right now—that will help you discern if you truly need to do more or buy more—is to ask God for His divine wisdom.

When you humbly ask God for wisdom, He will give it. In fact, His Word says so (James 1:5). Show that you affirm God's Word and teaching by asking for wisdom, and He'll show you just how much He affirms your prayers.

Father, I want to know that You are a happy parent toward me. I need Your wisdom in all that I do in preparation for this baby. Thank You for generously giving me wisdom.

The Praise of His Glory

In Him also we have obtained an inheritance, being predestined according to the purpose of Him who works all things according to the counsel of His will, that we who first trusted in Christ should be to the praise of His glory.

EPHESIANS 1:11–12 NKJV

During this mommy-to-be season of life, God affirms you—He upholds and supports you. Regardless of your past or the circumstances surrounding your pregnancy, He loves you! He is for you. When you commit your life to Him, you get to experience His blessings, share in His inheritance, and see Him use everything in your life for good.

Take some time to reflect on His affirmation toward you. Here are some ways to help you remember His commitment to you and your baby:

- Reflect on what life was like before this pregnancy. Was this baby a surprise? Or did you pray fervently for this baby? Thank God for answering your prayers to bless you with a baby. Pray that motherhood will deepen your faith and relationship with Him.

- Reflect on all of the wisdom, guidance, and counsel the Lord has blessed you with in these past few months. Praise God for providing you with the support you have needed.

Father, thank You for affirming me and our relationship. Thank You for providing me with a baby who will give me the opportunity to depend more on You.

His Children

See how very much our Father loves us, for he calls us his children, and that is what we are! But the people who belong to this world don't recognize that we are God's children because they don't know him.

1 JOHN 3:1 NLT

Annette felt huge. Tackling each daily task that once seemed easy made her feel like she needed a fifteen-minute cat nap. The thought of getting in the car with her two-year-old seemed like a daunting chore. But she knew it would be worth the effort to get out of the house and see other moms. These women were friends and mentors to her. She would also get free childcare and food!

So Annette asked the Holy Spirit to empower her with the physical and mental strength to enable her to get out the door and drive safely to church. On her way over, she turned on the radio and listened to some Christian music. That helped too.

As Annette parked, one of the leaders pulled into the spot next to her. She helped Annette get into the building, and she even helped get her two-year-old into the nursery. Annette was so thankful to God for providing everything she needed that morning. It reaffirmed to her that she truly was one of His children.

Father, thank You for the moments when I humbly pray and Your Holy Spirit empowers my ever-growing frame to do the impossible.

Make Merry

*The Lord appeared from of old to me (Israel), saying,
Yes, I have loved you with an everlasting love; therefore
with loving-kindness have I drawn you and continued My
faithfulness to you. Again I will build you and you will be
built, O Virgin Israel! You will again be adorned with your
timbrels (small one-headed drums) and go forth in the
dancing (chorus) of those who make merry.*
JEREMIAH 31:3–4 AMPC

Annette continued to see God answer her prayers at the moms' group. In her heart she silently prayed that God would strengthen her, fill her with His presence, and give her the encouragement she needed. With five weeks left to go, she felt weary, tired, and irritable. Her belly itched from all of the skin stretching, and she had to go to the bathroom every fifteen minutes. In her gut, she felt like this baby was going to come earlier than the expected due date.

As Annette made her way into the community room where the moms' group met, she saw some of her close friends flag her down—they'd saved a seat for her. She felt like God was reminding her that He was using these women to express His affirmation for her.

*Father, asking You for strength and encouragement
makes me merry, because then I get to watch You meet
my needs in ways that I couldn't do in my own strength!*

Everlasting Covenant

*"I will make an everlasting covenant with them: I will
never stop doing good to them, and I will inspire them to
fear me, so that they will never turn away from me. I will
rejoice in doing them good and will assuredly plant
them in this land with all my heart and soul."*
JEREMIAH 32:40–41 NIV

The Old Testament prophet Jeremiah told the Israelites about
the importance of the coming of God's new covenant that
would be found in Jesus Christ. God made a covenant with
their nation to love them, affirm them, and be with them. But
Jeremiah also reminded this nation that if they weren't humble
and obedient to God, they would face judgment.

So how is Jeremiah's message relevant to you, a mommy-
to-be? It's a reminder that God wants to support you and give
you everything you need. But His blessings of grace, mercy, and
goodness are magnified when you live a life committed to Him.

So take some time today to think about this everlasting
covenant that God made for you. He took care of it on the
cross when Jesus died at Calvary. Do you believe it? Of any
gift you receive before your baby arrives, this one is the most
important. Why? Because this can be what gives you peace
and stability that surpasses all understanding.

---

*Father, I commit my life to You. Thank You for using
the prophet Jeremiah to communicate a message
about the good news of Your saving grace.*

Worth

"Are not two sparrows sold for a penny? Yet not one of them will fall to the ground outside your Father's care. And even the very hairs of your head are all numbered. So don't be afraid; you are worth more than many sparrows."
MATTHEW 10:29–31 NIV

In Matthew 10 Jesus prepared His disciples for their commission to go out and preach the Good News. He charged them with several messages—some to encourage, some to inspire, some to bless, but all to support them and reinforce that they weren't alone in their God-given calling.

Jesus knew that these men had value and significance. He also knew they had weaknesses, but their weaknesses were a strength in that they would force them to depend fully on Christ, His teachings, and God's provision.

God has also called you as a mommy-to-be. You too are being commissioned to share the Good News with those who need it: your family, your baby, those you are interacting with leading up to the delivery of your child. Each of these people has worth in God's eyes.

So be empowered with the strength that comes only from the Holy Spirit to step out and share the Good News. You have nothing to be afraid of.

Father, even when I feel like I'm ready for this pregnancy to end, give me one more opportunity to witness to a child of Yours. You are worth it, and so are they.

WEEK 36

♡

Stretched

Your baby continues to pack on the pounds at about an ounce a day. While you might feel like your belly is physically stretched to the max, you are just a couple of weeks away from being considered full-term!

The Final Stretch

*God, the L*ORD*, created the heavens and stretched them
out. He created the earth and everything in it. He gives
breath to everyone, life to everyone who walks the earth.*
ISAIAH 42:5 NLT

Your due date is quickly approaching. Thanks to the infamous
nesting instinct, you may have gotten a lot done. Or you might
feel overwhelmed by all that's left to do.

But now more than ever is the time to remember that with
every poke and kick you feel, a miracle is living inside of you!

Yes, you are being stretched physically—and you might
have marks to prove it! You are being stretched emotionally
because of all the hormones raging inside of you. And you are
being stretched spiritually because God has chosen you, and
your body, to carry another one of His children into existence.

Ecclesiastes 11:5 (CEV) says, "No one can explain how a
baby breathes before it is born. So how can anyone explain
what God does? After all, he created everything."

So take a deep breath in. Then breathe out. As you do,
focus on the fact that since you were born, God gave you that
breath. Pretty soon you will witness your child's first breath of
life as well!

---

*Jesus, in these few moments that I'm taking for myself,
I choose to lean into Your peace. You are the giver
of breath and life, and I choose to focus on this
awesome creation moving inside of me.*

Called by Name

"And I have put my words in your mouth and hidden you safely in my hand. I stretched out the sky like a canopy and laid the foundations of the earth. I am the one who says to Israel, 'You are my people!'"
ISAIAH 51:16 NLT

Did you know that your name is significant? Have you ever looked up the meaning of your name? Often the name you have been given bears meaning that you will carry throughout the rest of your life.

For example, Jesus' name means "God will save." Isaiah's name means "Salvation of the Lord." Your name has a meaning too.

By now, if you know the gender of your child, you may have picked out a name for him or her. Or you might be starting to think about it.

Either way, pray and ask God for wisdom and insight concerning this child. What name does He want you to give His child? Take some time to research names that come to mind. And don't feel like you have to have a name picked out right before you go into labor. It's okay to go to the hospital with a few names. Then after delivery look at your baby, hold them for a bit after birth, get to know them and their temperament, and then decide.

Lord, You were called by name. You came into this world with purpose and a calling. Thank You that even I have a name that bears significance.

God Is in Control

*He has made the earth by His power, He has
established the world by His wisdom, and has
stretched out the heavens at His discretion.*
JEREMIAH 10:12 NKJV

Jeremiah is considered one of the Old Testament major prophets. His name means "God exalts." But it took Jeremiah a while to fulfill this high calling.

God called Jeremiah into a prophetic ministry at an early age, but Jeremiah resisted this call because he thought he was too young and inadequate. But God promised He would be with Him and that He would give Jeremiah the words to speak.

As a mommy-to-be, can you relate to Jeremiah? How many times have you felt inadequate and unfit for such a high calling? How many times have you felt out of control because of the demands (and hormones) that fill your day?

And then comes the all-consuming hope that God is with you. God is all you need. God is in control. Over and over again in the Bible there's proof that God is with you. In this moment, as you read these words, He loves you. Jesus is all you need.

---

*Lord, thank You for being my Father and Friend. Thank You
for being in control of this pregnancy. Even though I feel so
inadequate right now, help me to trust You. Help me to trust the
fact that You are on the throne as scripture says; You even care
about the details of this pregnancy.*

With All of My Heart

I will give thanks to you, LORD, with all my heart;
I will tell of all your wonderful deeds.
PSALM 9:1 NIV

This was Marie's second pregnancy. At week thirty-six she was feeling tired and uncomfortable. Sleep, which was once a plentiful commodity, was quickly becoming scarce due to her growing belly, pregnancy insomnia, and efforts to keep up with her preschooler.

Marie went in for her prenatal appointment and learned she had dilated and effaced significantly enough that she needed to modify her daily activities in order to rest. Anxiety filled her as she didn't want to deliver before full-term. Since Marie's husband worked from home and her three-year-old played throughout the house, she did her best to lie down and rest. Although it was boring to lie on the bed with her eyes wide open, she tried to look at it as an opportunity to praise God. As she did, her heart became grateful that her husband could work from home while she rested. She was aware that there was a baby inside of her and pretty soon they would get to meet.

Lord, I'm feeling uncomfortable, weary, and ready for this pregnancy to be over. Help me in these final weeks to stay focused on You and what Your Word says about me. Even though I feel like I'm walking through a valley, I will still praise You with all of my heart and soul.

Knitted Together

*You made all the delicate, inner parts of my body
and knit me together in my mother's womb.*
PSALM 139:13 NLT

Baby-soft skin. Chubby little legs. Beautiful eyes. Ten little fingers. Ten little toes. All jam packed into your lower abdomen. As the psalmist says, this baby has been knitted together in your womb.

David continued to write in Psalm 139:14–16 (NLT), "Thank you for making me so wonderfully complex! Your workmanship is marvelous—how well I know it. You watched me as I was being formed in utter seclusion, as I was woven together in the dark of the womb. You saw me before I was born. Every day of my life was recorded in your book. Every moment was laid out before a single day had passed."

Reflecting on this little life inside of you, take the time to say a prayer for him or her. Ask God to guide you and this child. Pray that your child may come to know Jesus at an early age. Pray for the days that God has ordained for them. That they may live out God's calling and purpose for their life, because it is He who knit them together inside your womb.

*Lord, thank You for bestowing upon me this precious gift.
This baby is a blessing from You. As You continue to
stretch me and knit my baby together inside of my womb,
help me to pray for this child every day of their life.*

A Reward

Children are a gift from the LORD;
they are a reward from him.
PSALM 127:3 NLT

Psalm 127 was written as a song for pilgrims traveling to Jerusalem. A song of praise, submission, and obedience to the Lord.

Becoming pregnant is a step of faith. It's a step of faith to trust that God will provide all of your needs and care for you and your family.

Family is an expression to the world of God's love. It is a witness, an invitation to accept God's unconditional love and grace. It's an opportunity for us to present to the world God's forgiveness and reconciliation. It's a high calling, a blessing, and a reward from the Lord.

Growing up, your family of origin may have been a safe haven, a support system that modeled God's love. Or perhaps your family of origin wasn't a safe place and caused you to fear and witness traumatic life events.

God doesn't discriminate based on your upbringing. He wants to continue creating people in His image. And He has chosen you to be a participant in the call to motherhood. Praise Him for rewarding you with this precious treasure!

Jesus, I sing praises to You for allowing me to be a mommy-to-be. I submit to Your will for my life with this child. Help me to care for my baby as an act of obedience to You. May people come to know You through my relationship with my child.

To Strengthen

*"Enlarge the place of your tent, and let them stretch
out the curtains of your dwellings; do not spare;
lengthen your cords, and strengthen your stakes."*
Isaiah 54:2 NKJV

Stretching occurs to strengthen. In order for new muscle fibers
to grow, old muscle fibers need to break down. Then the damaged muscle fibers create new, stronger muscle fibers.

During pregnancy a woman's body goes through a unique
process that affects every muscle group from the inside out.
Some women notice their bodies change at a rapid rate.
A once slender build now has a protruding belly and larger
breasts. These changes often leave us feeling out-of-sorts
after delivery, wondering when we will ever look and feel like
we did before pregnancy.

But if you look a bit deeper at a woman who just had a
baby, you'll notice something beautiful on the inside. While her
body has been enlarged to its maximum capacity, inside she
has been strengthened. Inside she has been refined because
her capacity to love and die to self has grown exponentially. To
the Lord this is most important. Man might look at the outward
appearance, but the Lord looks at the heart (1 Samuel 16:7).

*Heavenly Father, like Mary who bore Jesus, I am Your
bondservant. Help me to trust You with my body. As I reflect
on Isaiah 54:1–3, I thank You for blessing me with this child
and for growing my heart to love more like You do.*

WEEK 37

♡

Weaned

While baby's brain and lungs
continue to develop, your baby brain
moments might increase due to lack
of sleep and hormones. In addition,
you might feel like you can breathe
better if the baby starts to drop,
but you might also get winded
easier due to water retention
and weight gain.

Spiritual Milk

Like newborn babies you should crave (thirst for, earnestly desire) the pure (unadulterated) spiritual milk, that by it you may be nurtured and grow unto (completed) salvation, since you have (already) tasted the goodness and kindness of the Lord.
1 Peter 2:2–3 AMPC

The apostle Peter wrote to a group of Christians scattered among the northern areas of Asia Minor, where it's believed he may have previously shared the Gospel message.

As Peter wrote to these Christians, he reminded them how important it was to continually live out their faith. As we live out our faith, we will look different, but as believers we are all God's chosen people.

At thirty-seven weeks pregnant, you might feel like you need to cry one minute and scream the next. You might wonder when you will ever be able to bend properly, put lotion on your legs, shave your legs, or even see your legs. Yes, you are entering a part of the pregnancy that feels like a downward descent. A forty-week process is about to reach its grand finale.

Take some deep breaths. If you can go for a walk, do so. But most importantly, when all you feel like you can do is sit down and put your feet up, grab your Bible and drink in God's Word.

Father, I'm starting to feel like I can't do a whole lot. In these moments help me to remember that this is a great time to meditate on the pure spiritual milk of Your Word.

A Household Name

GOD, brilliant Lord, yours is a household name. Nursing infants gurgle choruses about you; toddlers shout the songs that drown out enemy talk, and silence atheist babble.
PSALM 8:1–2 MSG

Victoria was preparing for the last moms' group meeting for the school year. This meeting was also just a few days before Mother's Day. So at thirty-seven weeks pregnant, she wanted to do something that would honor each and every mom who attended.

Thankfully, in her third pregnancy, Victoria was feeling pretty good. She had one child who was in elementary school and another in preschool, so she was able to manage her moments of exhaustion a little more easily than during her previous pregnancies.

Sitting in a quiet house, Victoria typed up a devotional about how moms are called to make God a household name. She wrote that it was through leading the group that she learned so much about God, motherhood, and the power and presence of Jesus Christ in each meeting. It was her hope that their group meetings were enough to drown out enemy talk and babble and to refocus the women's attention on the goodness of their heavenly Father.

Lord, thank You for placing women in my life who have helped raise me up in such a way that I crave You more than anything else. Continue to help me depend on You and Your Word, being grateful for mentors who remind me to make You first in my life and home.

Within Me

*LORD, my heart is not proud; my eyes are not haughty.
I don't concern myself with matters too great or too
awesome for me to grasp. Instead, I have calmed and
quieted myself, like a weaned child who no longer cries for
its mother's milk. Yes, like a weaned child is my soul within
me. O Israel, put your hope in the LORD—now and always.*
PSALM 131:1–3 NLT

David asked the nation of Israel to always put their hope in
the Lord—to not put hope in themselves, but to put their hope
in God.

With three weeks left to go, where is your hope? Is it in the
doctors? What you have read? Other people's experiences with
labor and delivery? All of these things are good, but ultimately
God wants you to put your hope in Him. Like a weaned child
who no longer depends on their mother's milk, the Lord doesn't
want you to depend only on yourself or worldly perspectives.
All the encouragement and support you get is wonderful and
helpful. But ultimately, God is all you need. He created your
body for this season of life. Place your hope in Him.

*Father, I'm so grateful for all of the care You have
blessed me with. From friends and family to the medical
staff, I believe You have supplied everything I need
to have this baby. Ultimately, this life is in Your
hands. So help me to depend on You right now.*

Rejoice

Listen to your father, who gave you life, and do not despise your mother when she is old. Buy the truth and do not sell it—wisdom, instruction and insight as well. The father of a righteous child has great joy; a man who fathers a wise son rejoices in him. May your father and mother rejoice; may she who gave you birth be joyful!
PROVERBS 23:22–25 NIV

The word *wean* is defined as "to withdraw from some object, habit, form of enjoyment, or the like." By this point in your pregnancy, you might feel like you are being weaned from a lot of things you used to take for granted. For example, sleeping, eating a full meal, not running to the bathroom every fifteen minutes, being able to wear non-maternity clothes, being able to go out for long walks without getting winded or having Braxton Hicks contractions. Yes, there are a lot of enjoyments that you now realize you might have taken for granted.

But here's the blessing: you're almost done! In just a few more weeks you will get some of these things back. It's worth rejoicing that pretty soon you'll be giving birth and some of these symptoms will cease.

Father, I know that when I get back some of the things I've missed, like being able to see my feet, I'll be a mom. There's much to rejoice about because the end is in sight!

Pray It Through

*"Whatever you think is best," Elkanah agreed. "Stay here for now, and may the L*ORD *help you keep your promise."*
So she stayed home and nursed the boy until he was weaned. When the child was weaned, Hannah took him to the Tabernacle in Shiloh. They brought along a three-year-old bull for the sacrifice and a basket of flour and some wine.
1 SAMUEL 1:23–24 NLT

"When I had my first baby, I didn't want to put him in the nursery here at church until I weaned him," one of the mentors at the moms' group shared with Ruth, who was nervous about breastfeeding her first baby.

"For me, I just had a hard time with the idea of letting someone else give him a bottle. But you know what? With my second and third baby, it didn't matter anymore. I was okay with putting them in the nursery at a younger age regardless of whether they had been weaned or not."

Ruth was due in a few weeks, and she was trying to think about childcare options.

"Ruth, the most important thing you can do is just pray about it. Every baby is so different. Their needs are different, and your comfort level will be different too," the mentor encouraged her.

Father, as I'm starting to think about what to do after the baby is born, please give me sound wisdom and discernment. Make it clear to me what this baby's needs will be.

God's Plan

*But I will have mercy upon the house of Judah,
and will save them by the LORD their God, and will
not save them by bow, nor by sword, nor by battle,
by horses, nor by horsemen. Now when she had
weaned Loruhamah, she conceived, and bare a son.*
HOSEA 1:7–8 KJV

"One thing to remember, Ruth, is that when breastfeeding, some women don't get their period. And even though you might not get your period, you may still be fertile. Which means you can get pregnant," the mentor shared with her.

"Oh, right, I've heard about that," Ruth said.

"That happened to me within the first year of having my first baby. It wasn't the plan I had in mind. At first I felt overwhelmed. But then I got to see that it was a part of God's plan for my family, and eventually I had a peace about it. I think that's why God gives women nine months of pregnancy. It takes time to mentally prepare ourselves for everything that is in store."

Ruth appreciated the mentor's perspective and insight. She hoped that no matter what God's plan was for her as a mom, she would be willing to surrender control to God as the mentor did.

*Lord, I can plan and prepare all I want for this baby,
but I recognize that You have been in control since
conception and You will continue to be. I yield to You.*

A Great Feast

So the child grew and was weaned. And Abraham made
a great feast on the same day that Isaac was weaned.
GENESIS 21:8 NKJV

At this time in your pregnancy, the idea of a great feast might
sound a bit more like grazing on food throughout the day. But
there is one thought worth feasting on. As you look back over
the past thirty-seven weeks, have you witnessed a change in
your relationship with Jesus? Are you depending upon Him more
now than you ever were before? If your answer is yes, then this
is worth celebrating because you are weaning yourself off of
your dependence on yourself and leaning your dependence
more on God.

So what can a great spiritual feast look like these days,
especially when it's hard to eat a full meal in one sitting? Well,
how about taking some time alone with God. Go for a prayer
walk, journal, or do something else that will allow you to express
how God has been stretching your faith.

Father, I'm grateful that I can have a great feast with You! I
also look forward to the great feast that I will get to partake
in when I come home to be with You in heaven one day.
Thank You for using this pregnancy to help me lean less on
myself and more on You. Jesus, please keep me humble.

WEEK 38

♡

Delivered

Congratulations!
You're almost full-term!

Day of Delivery

He gives the childless woman a family,
making her a happy mother. Praise the Lord!
Psalm 113:9 nlt

At thirty-eight weeks pregnant, you might be starting to feel uncomfortable. Labor and delivery day is coming closer and closer, and the early days of pregnancy seem like a distant memory. . .or perhaps even a bit of a fog.

Now is a wonderful time to reflect on what it means to be delivered. Yes, soon you will be delivering a baby into this world. But what about when you became born again and entered a relationship with Jesus Christ? That day of delivery is just as much a milestone as the one that is to come in a few days or weeks.

In the days and weeks that followed the hallmark event of receiving Jesus into your heart, there have been other milestones of deliverance. Like when God pulled through for you and provided a breakthrough. Many women can attest to the fact that the day they found out they were pregnant was one of those hallmark moments. So in the middle of all that can come at thirty-eight weeks pregnant, praise Him and watch Him deliver your spirit and fill you with joy.

Father, right now I need to be delivered by Your
joy and peace. I know You can't remove all the
discomfort I'm feeling at this stage in my pregnancy.
But I do believe You can deliver me emotionally.
Please fill me with Your presence and peace.

Endurance

*Clothe yourselves therefore, as God's own chosen ones
(His own picked representatives), (who are) purified and holy
and well-beloved (by God Himself, by putting on behavior
marked by) tenderhearted pity and mercy, kind feeling,
a lowly opinion of yourselves, gentle ways, (and) patience
(which is tireless and long-suffering, and has the power to
endure whatever comes, with good temper).*
COLOSSIANS 3:12 AMPC

Paul encouraged the Christians in Colossae to keep the faith.
In their culture, there was an unease about accepting Jesus
Christ. It was an uncomfortable situation, but Paul endured.

With just a few more weeks left in your pregnancy, you
can relate to uneasiness and discomfort. At times you might
really wonder where God is in all of this. You might doubt that
He is really in control of all the details including your health
and body. Rest assured (although it may be hard to rest and
relax these days), God is in control and does see what you're
going through. Now is when you get to tap into what it means
to have an enduring faith. The Holy Spirit can deliver you from
this weariness and replace it with endurance. Just ask God and
watch what He will do in and through you!

*Father, in the moments when I want to give up
and I just want this baby out of me, please
give me endurance to wait on You.*

Compassionate

The LORD is compassionate and gracious, slow to anger, abounding in love. He will not always accuse, nor will he harbor his anger forever; he does not treat us as our sins deserve or repay us according to our iniquities. For as high as the heavens are above the earth, so great is his love for those who fear him; as far as the east is from the west, so far has he removed our transgressions from us.
PSALM 103:8–12 NIV

David writes in Psalm 103 about the greatness of God. David is surrendered to God's will. He is surrendered to God's forgiveness. He recognizes God's mercy and grace in his own life.

These days, whether you like it or not, you are surrendered to the process of pregnancy. You're surrendered to the process of creating another life and having your life changed along the way.

Have you told God how you feel lately? If not, take some time to do so. He wants to hear from you. Although He already knows your heart, He loves you and wants to hear your feelings and thoughts. You don't need to hold back; He can take it. He already did on the cross.

Father, You are compassionate even when I'm not. Pregnancy has been such a joy and such a consuming change in my life. I surrender to You. In my weakness please give me Your strength to express and receive Your compassion.

Once and for All

Beloved, while I was very diligent to write to you concerning our common salvation, I found it necessary to write to you exhorting you to contend earnestly for the faith which was once for all delivered to the saints.

JUDE 1:3 NKJV

Robin was excited to go to moms' group, but she was also nervous. In her second pregnancy, at thirty-eight weeks, she'd already started effacing and dilating. The worrier within her wanted to stay home, just in case she went into active labor. The optimist within her wanted to get out of the house and see her friends before delivery.

As Robin got into her sedan, she couldn't wait until she didn't have to constantly adjust the seat to accommodate her growing belly. As she started the car, she put on the radio. Robin heard a woman share about how she miscarried but then got pregnant and had a healthy baby. This put things in perspective for Robin. Even though she couldn't wait for certain pregnancy symptoms to be over, she praised God for giving her another gift of life.

Lord Jesus, once and for all I exalt You. I will sing a song of praise to You! Because of this new life, I will sing a new song! As Isaiah 42:14 (MSG) says: "I've been quiet long enough. I've held back, biting my tongue. But now I'm letting loose, letting go, like a woman who's having a baby."

Making an Appearance

And there appeared a great wonder in heaven; a woman clothed with the sun, and the moon under her feet, and upon her head a crown of twelve stars: and she being with child cried, travailing in birth, and pained to be delivered.
REVELATION 12:1–2 KJV

As Robin drove to moms' group, she played Christian music. Even though it was hard to breathe at times, she couldn't help but sing out loud. Fear that once consumed her about going into labor turned into great joy. Joy of knowing that just like the stoplight ahead of her, the finish line was in sight for this pregnancy.

As she made her way to church, she could feel a few twists and pokes coming from the baby. A reminder that her baby was still alive and kicking. A Braxton Hicks contraction came on as she parked the car in the parking lot, but it quickly subsided.

Reaching for her purse and cell phone, Robin checked her text messages. Several of her friends had sent her texts asking if she would be at the group that morning. Robin sent some quick replies back saying she'd be there and proceeded to waddle her way into the church.

Lord, thank You for giving me friends who understand what I'm going through. Thank You for mom groups that are not only a place for support and encouragement, but a place for friendship. Most of all, they help me to keep my focus on You!

A Firm Grip

It's crucial that we keep a firm grip on what we've heard so that we don't drift off. If the old message delivered by the angels was valid and nobody got away with anything, do you think we can risk neglecting this latest message, this magnificent salvation? First of all, it was delivered in person by the Master, then accurately passed on to us by those who heard it from him. All the while God was validating it with gifts through the Holy Spirit, all sorts of signs and miracles, as he saw fit.

HEBREWS 2:1–4 MSG

The writer of Hebrews acknowledged the importance of holding on to one's faith. The Word of God proved itself true through being taught, passed on, and confirmed through the Holy Spirit's power.

How do you hold on to your faith? By remaining focused on Jesus. How do you remain focused on Jesus? By keeping a firm grip on His words and teachings found in scripture.

In the days ahead, having a firm grip on your faith will help you get through this most crucial and life-giving part of pregnancy. Everything else around you may falter and fail, but the Word of God will stand true forever.

Jesus, when I feel myself slipping physically or emotionally, may You remain my constant source of stability and strength. Thank You for bringing me to the end of myself so that the only thing I have to hold on to is You and Your deliverance.

By Your Side

But the Lord stood at my side and gave me strength,
so that through me the message might be fully
proclaimed and all the Gentiles might hear it.
And I was delivered from the lion's mouth.
2 TIMOTHY 4:17 NIV

In his second letter to Timothy, the apostle Paul wrote to this young pastor to encourage and support his ministry. Paul, a mentor to Timothy, expressed how God delivered him and strengthened him to continue sharing the words of Jesus Christ.

Paul also wrote in 2 Corinthians 12:9–10 (NLT): "Each time he said, 'My grace is all you need. My power works best in weakness.' So now I am glad to boast about my weaknesses, so that the power of Christ can work through me. That's why I take pleasure in my weaknesses, and in the insults, hardships, persecutions, and troubles that I suffer for Christ. For when I am weak, then I am strong."

You can find great comfort today in knowing that when you feel weak during this pregnancy, you are actually strong. Because in your weakness you are poured out, depleted, and you can only find strength in Jesus.

Father, although in the next few weeks I'm going to give birth to a baby, You're also getting ready to deliver and birth something new within me! I can't wait to look back a few months from now and reflect on how You strengthened my faith during this tumultuous season of life.

WEEK 39

♡

Supported

Congratulations! You're full-term!

From Grief to Gladness

The proverbs of Solomon: A wise son makes a glad father, but a foolish and self-confident son is the grief of his mother.
PROVERBS 10:1 AMPC

As you get ready to have your child, take some time to reflect on your childhood. When do you remember making your parents glad? And what situations caused them grief? In the end, did they still express love and stability for you, despite your character?

This will be a constant parenting component to keep in check. There will be times that your delivered baby will do things that bring you great joy. There will be situations where they bring great frustration or even heartache. At the end of the day, you are called to love them and accept them just as they are, like God does you.

Here are some things to remember about God's character and love for you:

- He is with you always.

- He has never stopped loving you.

- He's your great provider, protector, and parent.

- He knows all of your needs.

- He wants to hear from you.

Father, thank You for Your unconditional love, mercy, grace, and forgiveness. As a mommy-to-be, prepare me to express these character traits to my baby. When those frustrating moments come, please give me the grace and strength to care for my child and give them what they need.

Training

Train up a child in the way he should go:
and when he is old, he will not depart from it.
PROVERBS 22:6 KJV

Solomon wrote some very wise words about parenting. Training up a child to love the Lord will stick with them. Though they might stray as an adult for a little while, they will remember the days of their youth. God will remind them of all they learned about Him. He will constantly pour out His love and affection on them. In essence, the wisdom found in this verse relates to sharing your faith with your child. How do you do this? It can start when they are born.

Be intentional about what you name your baby and pray about that name, because it may symbolize what they will live out. Praying over them when you rock them, feed them, or put them to sleep covers them with the mighty protection of God. It will train them to know the importance of prayer and dependence upon God.

In all that you say and do, your baby will grow up seeing how imperfect you are but how good God is in your life. They will see the reality of sinful human beings, as well as the humanity in which they live.

Father, as You have supported me, help me to support
this baby. Ultimately, I know that You are the best
parent they will ever have. So help me to stay humble,
meet their needs, and point them to You.

Let Them Come

Jesus said, "Let the little children come to me,
and do not hinder them, for the kingdom
of heaven belongs to such as these."
MATTHEW 19:14 NIV

Jesus loves little children. In fact, He loves the faith of little children. He supports their inquisitive spirits. Matthew 18:2–4 (NIV) says: "He called a little child to him, and placed the child among them. And he said: 'Truly I tell you, unless you change and become like little children, you will never enter the kingdom of heaven. Therefore, whoever takes the lowly position of this child is the greatest in the kingdom of heaven.' "

In gearing up to deliver this child, remember that you are also a child. Jesus' invitation isn't just for the young; it's for those who are older too. That includes you! So go to Him and ask Him to give you faith like a child. A humble and obedient faith, marked by His mercy and grace. He loves and supports you, and He will honor you for asking Him.

Father, if I could run right now I'd run to You the way a little child does to her parents. I'd embrace You the way that a child does. Thank You, Jesus, for accepting and supporting me just as I am. Thank You for loving me and calling me to be a mommy-to-be. I pray that in all I do I'm honoring You by being an expression of Your grace and mercy.

Whoever Receives

Then He took a little child and set him in the midst of them. And when He had taken him in His arms, He said to them, "Whoever receives one of these little children in My name receives Me; and whoever receives Me, receives not Me but Him who sent Me."
MARK 9:36–37 NKJV

In Mark chapter 9, Jesus explained to His disciples how to become great in His kingdom. The Twelve had been arguing about who was the greatest while on the road to Capernaum. This after Jesus predicted His death for the second time.

The disciples were looking for an answer and wanted to understand what He meant in predicting His death, but they were afraid to ask Him about it.

Jesus responded in kindness by making it clear who was the greatest. He said that anyone who wanted to be first must be last, and the servant of all. Then Jesus talked about receiving children—that to receive one in His name meant they also received Him and the One who sent Him.

Being a mommy-to-be and a child of God means that you get to witness to those around you, and they get to see that you are accepting this baby's life as one already loved by their Creator.

Father, I want to receive this little child with open hands and outstretched arms. I want to continue to receive You into my life in the same way. Thank You for receiving me.

Deep Reverence

This is the commandment, the rules and regulations, that
GOD, your God, commanded me to teach you to live out in
the land you're about to cross into to possess. This is so that
you'll live in deep reverence before GOD lifelong, observing
all his rules and regulations that I'm commanding you, you
and your children and your grandchildren, living good long
lives. Listen obediently, Israel. Do what you're told so that
you'll have a good life, a life of abundance and bounty, just
as GOD promised, in a land abounding in milk and honey.
DEUTERONOMY 6:1–3 MSG

Moses was trying to point out to the Israelites that God loved
and supported them. But did they support God? Did they show
their deep support and love for God by submitting to Him and
acting in obedience? If they did, God promised to bless them
abundantly.

You know that God loves and supports you, but where are
you with Him? On a scale of one to ten, with one being low
commitment to showing God reverence and ten being the
highest, where do you think you'd be? As a mommy-to-be,
you need Jesus in your life. Ask the Holy Spirit to empower you
with a deep reverence for God and His desires for your life.

Father, I want to live an abundant, obedient,
and faithful life. I need Your Holy Spirit's power to
show my devotion to You by living a deeply reverent life.

Not Yet Born

Our children will also serve him. Future generations
will hear about the wonders of the Lord. His righteous
acts will be told to those not yet born. They will
hear about everything he has done.
PSALM 22:30–31 NLT

In the weeks ahead and for the rest of your life, God has placed a very special calling on you as a mom. Each season, like this one, will look different. So what is the most important thing you can do for your child?

For you as a believer in Jesus Christ, the most important thing to do for your not-yet-born and soon-to-be-born children is to do what you are already doing: love Jesus. Show this love to your baby and to others. Share about who God is. Pray out loud and praise God, so that they may hear and see what it means to live out a life of faith. A faith that supports all that God is, and a faith that receives all of the love and support God has for you and them.

Father, I want to live out my faith before this baby when they are young and old. When I feel timid about sharing or expressing my love and devotion to You, please give me strength and the boldness that only comes from You.

Proclaim Your Power

Let each generation tell its children of your mighty acts;
let them proclaim your power. I will meditate on your
majestic, glorious splendor and your wonderful miracles.
PSALM 145:4–5 NLT

⌣

In Psalm 145, David both praised God and proclaimed His many attributes. This back-and-forth is a great representation of what a relationship with God looks like: fifty-fifty, a two-way street.

For some women, these last couple of weeks can be the hardest. There's a tension between wanting to be done with the pregnancy, wanting to greet your baby, and yet not looking forward to the change that is in store.

Now is a great time to grab your Bible and read out loud a psalm like Psalm 145. Read all twenty-one verses out loud, and as you do, invite God's presence to fill you. Watch as your mind recounts His goodness and faithfulness to you in these past few months. Then praise Him out loud for all of His goodness. If you want to take this a step further and you have the time and energy to do so, journal how you feel.

Also consider writing a letter to your baby. In it you can include God's goodness to you and them during this pregnancy. Write to them about what you're looking forward to doing when you first see them.

Father, show me how I can proclaim
Your goodness and power to my baby.

WEEK 40

♡

Held

It's time to say hello
and hold your baby!

Thrust into Your Arms

*Yet you brought me safely from my mother's womb
and led me to trust you at my mother's breast.
I was thrust into your arms at my birth. You have
been my God from the moment I was born.*
PSALM 22:9–10 NLT

In just a few short days you will get the chance to hold your baby!

Right now as you read this devotional, your heavenly Father is holding you. You might not feel it. You might not see it. But He is. Want proof? Look at how far He has helped you come during this pregnancy!

Take some time today to thrust yourself into His arms. What does thrusting yourself into His arms look like? You can read scripture. You can pray or sing worship songs. You can even close your eyes and believe by faith that you see Him holding you. He brought you safely from your mother's womb, and He has been your God since that moment. The very same moment that you are about to witness with your baby.

Father, You and I are about to witness a momentous occasion: my first time holding this precious baby. I'm looking forward to sharing this moment with You! Thank You for holding on to me.

Listen Up

*"Now therefore, listen to me, my children,
for blessed are those who keep my ways.
Hear instruction and be wise, and do not disdain it."*
Proverbs 8:32–33 NKJV

Wisdom. Wisdom is very important. Asking for wisdom is even more important. Acting on wisdom that comes from God is virtuous. Why? Because as the writer of Proverbs attests, wisdom calls for a humble heart and mind. A heart and mind that are willing to listen to God's instructions. In the end, there are blessings for those who hear His instructions and are wise. It's important not to treat God's wisdom and instruction with contempt.

You've made it this far in your pregnancy, and now more than ever you will continue to need to heed wisdom. Wisdom from God, from family members, from friends, and from your medical care team. When you feel like you're at your wit's end, don't turn from the wisdom and instruction God has been providing for you. God has good in mind for you with the biggest blessing of all: a baby to hold.

---

*Father, my hormones are raging, I'm tired, and I'm weary.
I'm also anxious to meet this baby. Please keep me humble
and obedient to You, Your Word, and Your instruction. Guide
me in the days ahead. When fear, worry, or pain seems too
much to take, I pray that Your grace, mercy, and peace
will fill in the gaps and be what I hold on to.*

Hold on Tight

"So now, with God as our witness, and in the sight of all Israel—the LORD's assembly—I give you this charge. Be careful to obey all the commands of the LORD your God, so that you may continue to possess this good land and leave it to your children as a permanent inheritance."

1 CHRONICLES 28:8 NLT

The writer of 1 Chronicles wanted the people of Israel to live lives devoted to God. In doing so, these people would receive blessings upon blessings as they held on tightly to God and His Word.

The same holds true for you as a mommy-to-be. God desires for you to finish this pregnancy strong. You might feel weak, but that's a good thing. This is an opportunity for God to be at His very best within you.

What does it look like for you to hold on tightly to God at forty weeks pregnant? Consider some of these ideas:

- Pray out loud.
- Sing out loud.
- Go for a walk, or a waddle, and talk to God out loud.
- Read your Bible.
- Call a friend and ask them to pray for you.
- Listen to a sermon.
- Listen to Christian music.
- Watch a faith-based movie.

Father, show me how to continue to hold on to You during these next few days. Thank You for using this pregnancy to build up and strengthen my faith. You are good, and I'm doing well because of what You have done.

His Peace

"*May the L*ORD *bless you and protect you. May the
L*ORD *smile on you and be gracious to you. May the
L*ORD *show you his favor and give you his peace.*"
NUMBERS 6:24–26 NLT

Moses shared with Israel God's blessings and faithfulness to them. Although God dearly loved them, Israel didn't always show their faithfulness to God.

This specific passage of scripture is a common one. Some refer to it as a benediction. Often you might hear a pastor recite it at the end of a church service or use it as a prayer.

Take some time today to pray this prayer over you and your baby. If you feel led to do so, ask your husband or a close family member to pray this over you too. Consider the words one at a time. Meditate on them, and as you do, envision God holding you close like a little girl He just doesn't want to let go of.

Father, hold me close to You. Even though I'm older and about to have a baby of my own to cuddle, please hold me close as a daddy holds his little girl. I need to know that You are holding me close. Thank You for blessing me. Thank You for protecting me. Thank you for smiling upon me. Thank You for being gracious to me. Thank You for showing me Your favor. Thank You for giving me Your peace.

Garland of Grace

Listen, my son, to your father's instruction and do not forsake your mother's teaching. They are a garland to grace your head and a chain to adorn your neck. My son, if sinful men entice you, do not give in to them.
PROVERBS 1:8–10 NIV

In Proverbs chapter 1, Solomon advises us to obey our parents' instructions and teachings. With obedience come beauty and grace that will stand out, provide a good life, and honor God.

As a mommy-to-be, you probably aren't thinking about the disciplines you'll have to instill in yourself and in your child as they grow older. After the baby comes, one of the most important things you can do is to provide them with a sense of comfort.

Holding your baby will create a unique bond. They will know instantly that you are their mom by the sound of your voice and by your touch. Hold them, rock them, and ask God to provide you with wisdom for each stage of this parenting journey.

Father, for now I'm looking forward to holding my baby—Your child. But in the months ahead, being a mom is going to take on a whole new dimension. Please provide me with Your wisdom and insight. I desire to live out Proverbs 20:7 (NLT), which says, "The godly walk with integrity; blessed are their children who follow them." May this child be a garland of grace.

A Promise to Hold On To

For I know the thoughts and plans that I have for you, says the Lord, thoughts and plans for welfare and peace and not for evil, to give you hope in your final outcome.
JEREMIAH 29:11 AMPC

Jeremiah shared with God's people about what was to come—the Messiah, the state of their nation, and God's love for them.

Jeremiah 29:11 is a familiar passage of scripture often referred to at or around major milestones in one's life.

As a mommy-to-be, you can hold on to the promise in this passage. The New Living Translation puts it this way: " 'For I know the plans I have for you,' says the LORD. 'They are plans for good and not for disaster, to give you a future and a hope.' "

What is this promise? A hope and a future; plans for good and not for disaster.

To look a little bit more closely, here's the New International Version's translation of this verse: " 'For I know the plans I have for you,' declares the LORD, 'plans to prosper you and not to harm you, plans to give you hope and a future.' "

Plans that will prosper and not harm you. There's life and hope in these words. A promise that you can hold on to as you wait for your baby to arrive.

Father, help me to believe by faith that
You have plans for my good and Your glory.

Gather with His Arm

He shall feed his flock like a shepherd: he shall gather
the lambs with his arm, and carry them in his bosom,
and shall gently lead those that are with young.
ISAIAH 40:11 KJV

Isaiah, an Old Testament prophet, spoke about the coming of Jesus Christ. The Messiah would be a shepherd to His people—that's you. Jesus carries you like a lamb in His bosom and He gently leads you. Jesus is holding on to you.

So here you are, mommy-to-be. The end of a forty-week calling and season in your life. A journey to new life, from conception to birth. Throughout this pregnancy you have had the opportunity to be reminded of God's love for you, His promises, and most of all His presence with you! Reading scripture daily has become a habit worth holding on to, because you will need to depend on Jesus throughout motherhood.

Father, help me to continue to hold on to and depend upon
You. Although I might be tempted to follow my own plans,
my own thoughts or wisdom, help me to go to You and Your
Word first. Help me to trust Your promise in Isaiah 66:13 (NIV):
"As a mother comforts her child, so will I comfort you."
Thank You for holding on to and comforting me!

About the Author

Stacey Thureen desires to help women stay grounded in their faith so that they can find stability on the seesaws of life. Her writing includes contributions to *Daily Wisdom for Women* devotional collections published by Barbour Books. When Stacey isn't writing or speaking, she enjoys swimming and spending time with family. Connect with her at www.StaceyThureen.com.

Scripture Index